George Orwell Studies

Volume Four

No. 1

George Orwell Studies

Publishing Office
Abramis Academic
ASK House
Northgate Avenue
Bury St. Edmunds
Suffolk
IP32 6BB
UK

Tel: +44 (0)1284 700321
Fax: +44 (0)1284 717889
Email: info@abramis.co.uk
Web: www.abramis.co.uk

Copyright
All rights reserved. No part of this publication may be reproduced in any material form (including photocopying or storing it in any medium by electronic means, and whether or not transiently or incidentally to some other use of this publication) without the written permission of the copyright owner, except in accordance with the provisions of the Copyright, Designs and Patents Act 1988, or under terms of a licence issued by the Copyright Licensing Agency Ltd, 33-34, Alfred Place, London WC1E 7DP, UK. Applications for the copyright owner's permission to reproduce part of this publication should be addressed to the Publishers.

© 2019 George Orwell Studies & Abramis Academic

ISSN 2399-1267
ISBN 978-1-84549-753-8

George Orwell

Contents

Rebel? Prophet? Relic? New Perspectives on Orwell

Guest Editorial
Orwell's Enduring Appeal – by Sarah Gibbs   Page 3

Keynote
Orwell, My 'Orwell' – by John Rodden   Page 6

Papers
Red Flags, Black Ties: Orwell's Anarchist Sympathies and *The Conquest of Bread* in Spain – by Dana Wight   Page 13

Surveillance From Orwell to *Orwell*: The Power of Vision in Popular Culture – by Xiaozhou Li   Page 27

The Unconscious on Screen: Psychoanalytic Themes in Michael Radford's adaptation of *Nineteen Eighty-Four* – by James Jarrett   Page 43

Plus

Papers
The Politics of the Uncanny: George Orwell and the Paranormal – by Philip Bounds   Page 57

Nineteen Eighty-Four, the Secret State and the Julia Conundrum – by Richard Lance Keeble   Page 71

Articles
Memoirs of Orwell: The Quest for the Truth – by Jeffrey Meyers   Page 85

Barnhill: A Labour of Love – by Norman Bissell   Page 98

Leon Gellert, George Orwell and *Nineteen Eighty-Four* – by Darcy Moore   Page 105

1984 in 2020: The Deeper Concerns – by Tom Cooper   Page 113

Reviews
Alexis Pogorelskin on *Dzhordzh Oruell: Biografiya* [George Orwell: Biography] by Masha Karp, Desmond Avery on *Sur les Traces de George Orwell*, by Adrien Jaulmes and Richard Lance Keeble on *Barnill: A Novel*, by Norman Bissell   Page 117

Editors
Richard Lance Keeble — University of Lincoln
Tim Crook — Goldsmiths, University of London

Reviews Editor
Megan Faragher — Wright State University

Production Editor
Paul Anderson — University of Essex

Editorial Board
Kristin Bluemel — Monmouth University, New Jersey
Peter Marks — University of Sydney
John Newsinger — Bath Spa University
Marina Remy — Paris Sorbonne
John Rodden — University of Texas at Austin
Jean Seaton — University of Westminster
Peter Stansky — Stanford University, US
D. J. Taylor — Author, journalist, biographer of Orwell
Florian Zollmann — Newcastle University

EDITORIAL

Orwell's Enduring Appeal

SARAH GIBBS

I recently chaired a panel at the '*1984* Now' symposium in Oxford during which Anna Vaninskaya and Dorian Lynskey discussed the challenges of teaching Orwell's works at university. One attendee wondered how to 'defamiliarise' his final novel and engage students who feel they already know all about Big Brother. Lynskey, whose new book, *The Ministry of Truth: A Biography of George Orwell's 1984*, considers the text's germination and afterlife, advised that instructors focus on the author's flaws and eccentricities. To find the work anew, he contended, readers must shatter the image, must topple the statues to Orwell the Prophet, Orwell the Saint.

I have often felt that the author of the twentieth century's most famous dystopia has suffered the fate he himself assigned to Charles Dickens: he is widely known at second hand. The degree to which *Nineteen Eighty-Four*'s (1949) characters and neologisms have permeated public discourse means that not only students but also academics often view the text itself as superfluous. I recall one member of the faculty at a North American institution confiding to me: 'I'd love to work on Orwell, but there just doesn't seem to be anything there. He's already been digested.' The conference that I organised at University College London (UCL) in May 2019, a number of papers from which appear in this issue of *George Orwell Studies*, was part of my effort to refute that scholar's assumption and to offer evidence that the 'wintry conscience of a generation' produced not only the linguistic shorthand we use to describe state oppression but also a rich and rewarding literature.

'Rebel? Prophet? Relic? Perspectives on George Orwell in 2019' took place on 24-25 May and featured papers from academics and Orwell enthusiasts from across the globe. I had two primary objectives in assembling panels. Firstly, I sought presentations that could recontextualise the author and his *oeuvre*, placing Orwell within the greater mid-century narrative and making legible the allusions and satire which feature so prominently in his works. Dana Wight's 'Red Flags, Black Ties: Orwell's Anarchist Sympathies and *The Conquest of Bread*' uses the book by the Russian thinker and

Sarah Gibbs

political activist, Peter Kropotkin, to reassess Orwell's association with anarchism, a connection too often dismissed, Wight argues, as 'exaggeration or misattribution'.

My second goal in programming the conference was, as the event's title suggests, to interrogate our contemporary deployment of Orwell's name and ideas, and to consider his legacy in the twenty-first century. John Rodden, the world's foremost authority on Orwell's reception history and the conference's keynote speaker, has penned for this issue 'Orwell, My "Orwell"'. The piece turns on a possibility. Rodden writes:

> Perhaps to an extent even greater than that of [Dr.] Johnson, the enduring power of this figure 'Orwell' consists not so much in what he wrote as in what he was – or rather 'became'. Or still better: is *perceived* to have become.

The distance between Orwell and 'Orwell' is considerable. James Jarrett's paper examines how Michael Radford's film treatment of *Nineteen Eighty-Four* has enriched our perception of both writer and text. In Xiaozhou Li's 'Surveillance from Orwell to *Orwell*: The Power of Vision in Popular Culture', the 1949 novel is the source of a rich symbolic and linguistic imaginary on which artists draw in order to portray surveillance culture.

I am put in mind of a scene in A. S. Byatt's Booker Prize-winning novel, *Possession* (1990), when her literary scholar protagonist justifies his love for a Victorian writer's work: '[The poems] were what stayed alive, when I'd been taught and examined everything else.' That Orwell's texts have survived not only the education system, but also an otherwise unprecedented absorption into popular culture, is a profound testament to their quality, and a compelling reason to eschew a 'second hand' acquaintance in favour of the real thing.

Happy reading!

Sarah Gibbs,
PhD candidate,
UCL Department of English Language and Literature

- Richard Lance Keeble and Tim Crook add: Luke Seaber has decided to step down from his position as Reviews Editor of *George Orwell Studies*. We would like to express our sincere thanks to him for carrying out the role with such panache since the launch of the journal in 2016: the quality of the reviews he has secured has always been impressive and his wide range of contacts has helped give the journal a distinct international edge. His place is taken by Megan Faragher, Associate Professor at Wright State University's Lake Campus. Her research explores the intersection of propaganda, social psychology, and twentieth-century British literature. She has contributed essays to the journals including *Textual Practice, The Space Between Journal,* and *Literature & History* as well as essays in several edited collections, including *Twenty-First Century Literature and the City* and *Humans at Work in the Digital Age: Forms of Digital Textual Labor*. We are sure Megan will bring her own expertise and contacts to the role – and we look forward to working with her. Finally, another welcome to the editorial board for Professor John Rodden, visiting scholar at the Harry Ransom Research Center, University of Texas at Austin and the leading authority on the global reception of Orwell's works.

KEYNOTE

Orwell, My 'Orwell'

Orwell is the most important writer since Shakespeare and the most influential writer who has ever lived. So argues John Rodden in his keynote speech to the UCL conference – in which he also explores the origins of his own fascination with the man: his life and letters, his legend and legacy.

WHY DO I THINK ABOUT ORWELL SO OFTEN AND WRITE SO MUCH ABOUT HIM?

I ask myself that question periodically. For although I have written books on American and European public intellectuals, the English novel, the politics of culture in Germany, Latin American fiction, the literary interview, human rights abuses, comparative education, comparative communist and capitalist education and other topics, I have always returned to Orwell. His life and letters, his legend and legacy, have all preoccupied me. My answer as to 'Why George Orwell?' is simply that, ever since I first opened his books, I have always felt a powerful connection with him and with particular aspects of his thought and literary personality or persona.

I am also well aware that I consider myself one of Orwell's junior 'literary siblings' and regard him as an 'intellectual big brother' (not Big Brother!), per the title of my book *Every Intellectual's big brother: George Orwell's Literary Siblings* (2006). I mention that because the role of 'older brother' implies a chronological gap, or in the metaphorical sense that I apply it to Orwell, a bridge between generations.

In fact, much of a person's response to any elder has to do with his or her generational relationship. This is also true with respect to a writer, as I discovered in conducting numerous interviews both with Orwell's old friends and acquaintances and with several of his immediate intellectual contemporaries who responded to him as generational coevals during his own life. By contrast, I am two or three generations removed not only from Orwell's era but even from the posthumous publication of his writings, most of which appeared by the mid-1950s, before I was born.

As a result, by the time I embarked on a serious inquiry into Orwell's *oeuvre*, the scholarly ground had already been well tilled. By the mid-1980s, more than three decades after his death, his books had sold in the tens of millions in five-dozen languages, and I beheld a Brobdingnagian spectre ('Call me "Orwell"') bestriding the planet and dwarfing (and overshadowing) the now-famous man of letters.

The writer George Orwell had become a world-historical figure, but the ever-lengthening ('Orwellian') shadow of 'Orwell' had become far more visible and widely known. And so the critical task was at least as much to make sense of his Work, of the unique phenomenon of 'Orwell', as it was the investigation and interpretation of his writings themselves.

FROM BLAIR TO ORWELL TO 'ORWELL'

My point here is that historical timing induced me to make 'Orwell', even more so than George Orwell, the focus of my work decades ago – and the media attention riveted ever after on this spectral presence has continued to direct my own critical inquiries during the last 30-odd years. For if the analysis of his writings had already reached a very sophisticated and, in certain areas, near-definitive status by the early 1980s, this was not at all true of 'Orwell' as a literary icon, cultural symbol and political talisman.

No scholar or intellectual had closely investigated his outsized reputation. In my first book, *The Politics of Literary Reputation*, published in 1989, I set myself this challenge: to discuss not only Orwell's writings but also the phenomenon of 'Orwell'. 'If you want to understand Orwell,' Richard Rees once remarked, 'you have to understand Blair.' Even more so, I would contend: if you want to understand 'Orwell', you have to understand Orwell. And so, while much has been written about the process of 'Eric Blair' becoming 'George Orwell' (one biography refers to it, in its subtitle, as 'The Transformation'), the following pages discuss what might be called the transmogrification of Orwell into 'Orwell'. This is a much bigger, more far-reaching and more nebulous matter, virtually unbounded in scope, as a series of studies I have conducted about the history of Orwell's reputation and impact in the modern world attest. Indeed, I might title them *Orwell Unbound*, or rather *'Orwell' Unbound*, thereby highlighting the immense, incalculable and seemingly measureless character of the reception and influence of 'Orwell'.

THE 'GREATNESS' OF THE MAN?

And yet: might it be that the genius of Blair-Orwell is not to be found, at least not chiefly, in his writings, whether fiction or nonfiction? A case can be made that the greatness of Orwell was in the man whose originality and uniqueness inspired a wide circle of friends and acquaintances to apotheosise him almost immediately upon his death. This is another sense in which we can speak of

John Rodden

'Orwell'. In this characterisation, the quotation marks refer not to a bogeyman, but to a literary figure 'transfigured' by those who met him, the figure of 'George Orwell' in all of his endearing eccentricities (his love of schoolboy papers such as boys' weeklies), odd-man-out oddities (the acrid, shag cigarettes that he proudly rolled himself), and outlandish proclamations ('All tobacconists are fascists!').

In saying all this, I reverse the judgment of Bernard Crick in the pioneering first biography of Orwell: 'The work is greater than the man.' Certainly a touch of genius is there in the books, especially in *Animal Farm* and *Nineteen Eighty-Four*, and arguably in *Homage to Catalonia* and several of the brilliant essays. Yet it strikes me forcefully, on turning from the books to the memories of those who met Blair-Orwell, whether they loved or hated him, that his literary gifts represent only a fraction of his curriculum vitae. And in that connection I am reminded of a cautionary warning voiced by Paul Valéry. In his essay 'Descartes', he wrote:

> My own view is that we cannot really circumscribe a man's life, imprison him in his ideas and his actions, reduce him to what he appeared to be and, so to speak, lay siege to him in his works. We are much more (and sometimes much less) than what we have done.

Any literary historian or biographer must ponder this insight, for it should weigh heavily in any assessment of a person's conduct and achievement, especially in those cases (such as that of Orwell) in which posthumous history seems vastly at odds with the life that was lived.

I mention all this because, having studied so closely – and interviewed whenever possible the responses of admirers (and adversaries) of Orwell – I take issue with Bernard Crick's confident claim. Certainly Orwell's work does not capture or convey all of him, perhaps above all not the loveable, quixotic, humorous, obtuse, crotchety comrade whom friends cherished and foes scorned. For Orwell stands, as A. N. Wilson once wrote of a very different writer and thinker, Hilaire Belloc, 'at the opposite end of the spectrum from Shakespeare, a genius wholly subsumed in his work and whom, by all accounts, "gave" little in actual meeting'. Orwell was much more like Dr Johnson, whom Wilson also places at the Belloc pole as a man who was mythologised 'by his intimates' even though he, too, composed 'not one literary work by which this belief could be sustained'. Perhaps to an extent even greater than that of Johnson, the enduring power of this figure 'Orwell' consists not so much in what he wrote as in what he was – or rather 'became'. Or still better: is *perceived* to have become.

So 'Orwell' is not just a matter of haunting catchwords and horrifying nightmare visions. It is equally, if not more so, about the man whom we have caricatured and canonised. In this sense 'becoming George Orwell' is also fundamentally about the process of what could be called 'figuration'. Or, as his friend Malcolm Muggeridge wrote in a diary entry shortly after Orwell's death, marvelling at the memorial tributes to and growing reputation of 'George', the story of Orwell's afterlife is also about 'how the legend of a human being is created', about how a man 'becomes' a myth. It is both fortunate and unfortunate that Orwell was memorialised not by one Boswell but by several well-intentioned yet partial memoirists – among them Muggeridge, Julian Symons, George Woodcock, Tosco Fyvel, Cyril Connolly, Bertrand Russell, Stephen Spender and Richard Rees. They have all bequeathed us vivid portraits of the author as a middle-aged man.

FREELANCING IN THE FOOTSTEPS OF 'ST. GEORGE'

Not only for me but also for many of my peers and elders, Orwell has seemed 'every intellectual's big brother'. Decades earlier I had already discovered that I was simply following in a long line of impassioned readers, whether enthusiasts or enemies. In *Every Intellectual's big brother: George Orwell's Literary Siblings* – let me emphasise here again that the lowercase usage is meant to specify Orwell rather than 'Orwell'– I described how other intellectuals have responded to Orwell and how we are all part of a literary family. My own stirring and powerful attraction to Orwell, both his life and his *oeuvre*, eventually led me to study the writing of his admirers and even his antagonists. I found myself ardently drawn to those who esteemed Orwell, albeit often at a different historical moment and for different reasons than myself, such as the group of New York intellectuals associated with *Partisan Review* between the 1930s and 1990s, one of whom (Dwight Macdonald) became personally acquainted with Orwell through extensive correspondence. I began to interview and write about many of these generational peers of Orwell who were my own American intellectual elders. If I could not meet Orwell personally, I could at least get to know them. I could, in fact, visit and get to know them far more easily than I could Orwell's ageing British colleagues across the Atlantic.

On a more personal (or more visceral) level, I feel a special affinity with Orwell because I identify with his battle, like my own, to become an independent writer and intellectual. That struggle has never been easy, but it is even more difficult today than it was in Orwell's time, because the Western academy has swallowed up intellectual life and regurgitated academic specialists, most of whom do not write for the public or in an accessible idiom. There is no institution – whether in the form of PhD or creative writing programmes or law schools or think tanks – that forms intellectuals. Today as ever – all the certification bodies, credentialing institutions,

KEYNOTE

John Rodden   MFA workshops and graduate and postgraduate fellowship programmes notwithstanding – the vocation of the intellectual can only be pursued and practised in the time-honoured way that, assisted by his generational ancestors, Orwell also followed. What way is this? Sustained by yearning and will, you immerse yourself in the work of those who have gone before you and who have become serious writers and intellectuals themselves.

Or, as I put it in *Every Intellectual's big brother*, you 'adopt' an intellectual big brother or big sister. You ingest his or her work as a way of realising your own best self as a writer and human being. Orwell had the advantage of belonging to a large London literary community supported by numerous little magazines and intellectual quarterlies. Nowadays, these urban communities, whose hubs were typically literary reviews or cultural quarterlies, have almost vanished. The university has replaced them with remunerative employment that is far more comfortable yet forms a very different creature than the traditional intellectual. I have written about this shift in my forthcoming *The Intellectual Species: Evolution or Extinction?* In this book, I describe how the 'species' of the traditional literary intellectual, who addresses the broader public on issues of common national and international concern, is gravely endangered today. The rise of the adjective 'public' – as in 'public' intellectual – has coincided with (and, indeed, confirmed) the death of the species.

Decades ago, one never needed to distinguish between a 'public' intellectual and other kinds of intellectuals. But now that the academic or the policy intellectual – the resident species of higher education institutions or Washington think-tanks – dominates the scene, a sea change has occurred: a loose fish swimming freely against the nets that would hold him (such as in Melville's *Moby Dick*) and speaking out to the wider public on diverse issues of common interest is all too uncommon.

I have embraced Orwell warmly, if also gingerly and cautiously, as an intellectual big brother. I once wrote an open letter to voice my debt to him and explain why I have devoted such a substantial part of my life and intellectual energy to him and his heritage. I began to realise in the 1990s that I had adopted Orwell as my intellectual big brother as a way of discovering and resolving my own issues of personal identity as a writer and aspiring intellectual. Orwell came into my life at a moment when my needs and dreams could be clarified by glimpsing the Orwell in myself, that is, by seeing how we were, indeed, brothers of a different generation, elder and (very) junior men of letters. I first valued him for his political acumen and moral example, as have countless other readers, especially his willingness to swim against the prevailing currents ('My Orwell, Left or Right'). Later, I came to cherish the whimsical, quirky, (almost) perversely eccentric, inimitably quixotic figure of lore in the memorial tributes of his friends ('My Orwell, Deft or Trite').

If I have also devoted myself not just to the man and writer, but also to 'Orwell' and to his Work – and, thus, to the author's literary and political legacy – I discern that this decision also has had to do with his influence on me which, in some respects, is indirect and even oblique. For Orwell has exerted a powerful influence on wide-ranging developments in culture, society and politics throughout my lifetime. My identification with him, and my fascination with his unique legacy, is a tacit acknowledgment that he has become a world-historical individual, what Jean-Paul Sartre referred to as a 'singular universal', a rare being whose existential trajectory (inadvertently?) situates him at a historical crossroads where he somehow manages to touch on universal concerns through his singular life.

THE EFFLUENCE OF HIS INFLUENCE

Orwell is the most important writer since Shakespeare and the most influential writer who has ever lived. Quite a bold claim! Let me clarify it, if not qualify it. I do not say that he is the greatest imaginative writer, nor even the leading novelist of his generation. I do not even mean that he is the bestselling writer of all time. I make no exalted claims for the intrinsic quality of his work versus that of other writers. Rather, I'm speaking simply about his shaping influence of his language, vision and liberal vision on the post-World War II world – the effluence of his influence. No English-language writer in recent generations has aroused so much controversy and inspired so many younger writers and intellectuals. Certainly no one before or after Orwell has contributed so many incessantly quoted words and phrases to our cultural lexicon. (One has to reach back to Dickens and even Shakespeare to cite any comparable analogues – and those are near-exclusively English-language, indeed, chiefly British, examples at that.) Orwell's very name as a proper adjective is quoted in numerous languages tens of thousands of times per year. Moreover, his appeal both to serious readers and to academics and intellectuals – his 'literary bandwidth', as it were – knows no comparison. It is in these respects that I use the phrases 'most important' and 'most influential'.

I should add here that the casual observations of numerous political journalists and social commentators implicitly support my claim. For instance, although in his best-selling *Churchill and Orwell: The Fight for Freedom* (London: Penguin, 2017), two-time Pulitzer Prize-winner Thomas E. Ricks gives Churchill top billing, he remarks: 'In recent years, [Orwell] may have even passed Churchill, not in terms of historical significance but of cultural influence.' If not Orwell, I would contend, 'Orwell' has certainly done so – in fact, decades ago and on both counts.

John Rodden I was not alive either when he lived or when most of his posthumous work was published in the first post-World War II decade. As the year 1984 crept ever nearer and the 'countdown' mentality took hold, however, I witnessed with fascination the rise of the world-historical 'Big O', that ever-looming leviathan that incarnated the severely abridged, sensationalised Work and came to be represented by the master sign 'Orwell' and mobile-missile metaphor 'Orwellian'. Of course, 'Orwell' is a double-edged sword. This is the bogeyman behemoth, the 'Orwellian' spectre of *Nineteen Eighty-Four*, the Big Brother who is quoted and misquoted in legions of contexts. Both the Work and 'Orwell' (or 'Orwellian') have been invoked *ad nauseam* in contemporary discussions about the invasions of Afghanistan and Iraq, Saddam Hussein and Vladimir Putin (and Donald Trump and Barack Obama) and so on.

'Orwell' possesses a dark, sometimes raven black, side but I have been concerned with both the darkness and the light; that is, the full palette of the literary legacy – the iridescent, multi-coloured portraits as well as the sketches in sepia gracing the gallery in all their wondrous variety and ambiguity. 'Orwell' can be used for positive ends, but typically he has been abused for ends that the man and writer would never have endorsed and perhaps never even have imagined. Surely George Orwell would have objected to the monochromatic view of him as a Cold War Warrior and even more fiercely, as he did late in his lifetime, to his reputation in some quarters as an anti-socialist.

I have sought to clarify with scholarly accuracy his legacy and not to indulge in the practice of robbing his grave or moving his coffin to the left or to the right for my own political purposes. I readily grant, however, that every person has his or her blind spots and biases. And so I have always aimed both to declare and explain my own interests and convictions, thereby to render my 'colour filter' discernible so that the reader may know: *Caveat lector!*

That knowledge is indispensable. So forewarned, the reader – in this case, my readers – may notice my blind spots as well as my insights. And thereby notice how I inevitably, inescapably (re)construct my storied Orwell – and 'Orwell' – through the lens of my own history and subjectivity.

- This essay is based on the keynote address delivered at the George Orwell Symposium at University College London in May 2019. John Rodden has written several books on the work and heritage of George Orwell, including *George Orwell, Life and Letters, Legend and Legacy,* forthcoming from Princeton University Press.

PAPER

Red Flags, Black Ties: Orwell's Anarchist Sympathies and *The Conquest of Bread* in Spain

DANA WIGHT

George Orwell opens Homage to Catalonia, *his 1938 memoir of the Spanish civil war, with the description of an Italian militiaman enlisted with the Spanish anarchists; he later commemorates the man in a poem (1943) honouring his 'crystal spirit'. Though Orwell did not identify himself as an anarchist during the war, and his political position cannot be more concretely defined than anti-fascist, the esteem he holds for this militiaman exemplifies the political ideals he shared with the Spanish anarchists. This paper examines Orwell's anarchist sympathies and his commitment to the politics of 'common decency' through the framework of Russian anarchist theorist Peter Kropotkin's foundational text* The Conquest of Bread *(1892) and considers the ways in which these politics extend to Orwell's later political affinities.*

Keywords: anarchism, anti-fascism, Spain, revolution, decency

INTRODUCTION

In late 1936, following the military uprising in Spain led by Francisco Franco and supported by fascist governments in Germany and Italy, George Orwell travelled to Barcelona to fight alongside the anarchist and Marxist-communist revolutionaries in the Spanish civil war. Orwell opens *Homage to Catalonia*, his 1938 memoir of the war, with the description of an Italian militiaman standing at the front of the officers' table in the Lenin Barracks. He writes:

> Something in his face deeply moved me. It was the face of a man who would commit murder and throw away his life for a friend – the kind of face you would expect in an Anarchist ... I have seldom seen anyone – any man, I mean – to whom I have taken such an immediate liking. ... With his shabby uniform and fierce pathetic face he typifies for me the special atmosphere of that time. He is bound up with all my memories of that period of the war (2001 [1938]: 31).

DANA WIGHT

Orwell's impression of this man stayed with him long after the war and publication of his memoir – he revisits the encounter in his essay 'Looking Back on the Spanish War' (1943) which includes a poem he wrote in the militiaman's honour. The poem's final lines are: 'But the thing I saw in your face/No power can disinherit:/No bomb that ever burst/Shatters the crystal spirit' (2001 [1943]: 363). In the essay, Orwell reiterates that 'This man's face, which I saw for only a minute or two, remains with me as a sort of visual reminder of what the war was really about': namely, 'the attempt of people like this to win the decent life which they knew to be their birthright' (ibid: 360).

Though Orwell did not identify himself as an anarchist during the war, and his political position cannot be more concretely defined than anti-fascist, the esteem he holds for this militiaman exemplifies the political ideals he shared with the Spanish anarchists. He states in his memoir that 'If you had asked me why I had joined the militia I should have answered: "To fight against Fascism", and if you had asked me what I was fighting *for*, I should have answered: "Common decency"' (Orwell 2001 [1938]: 169). He later echoed this sentiment in a letter to his friend and biographer George Woodcock, in which he wrote that 'human society must be based on common decency' (as cited in Feaver 1994: 8). George Woodcock, who was notably an anarchist himself, titled his biography of Orwell *The Crystal Spirit,* after the final line in Orwell's poem about the Italian militiaman, and notes within that he spent his life dedicated to the principles of 'brotherhood, fair play and honest dealing' (Woodcock 1966: 28). Orwell's sympathies are consistently with those who are underprivileged and disenfranchised by bourgeois capitalism. His steadfast commitment to the politics of 'common decency' and to the 'decent life' people like the Italian militiaman were fighting for, aligns with the fundamental tenets of anarchism – particularly those established by the nineteenth-century Russian anarchist Peter Kropotkin.

ORWELL'S ANARCHISM

In its barest form, anarchism is an ideology based upon the principles of social equality and individual freedom, the human inclination towards peace and cooperation and the rejection of an authoritarian state. Following revolutionary nineteenth-century studies in biology and evolution, anarchist thinkers such as Kropotkin denied the Hobbesian 'state of nature' and rejected misappropriated theories of social Darwinism, arguing instead that human beings, as with any social animal, must develop systems of trust and cooperation in order to ensure their survival as a species. These systems are founded on collectivist, communitarian principles of social organisation: the practices of 'mutual aid' form the basis of anarchism, or what Kropotkin defines as 'the No-Government system of Socialism' (Kropotkin 1895 [1887]: 3, capitals in the original).[1] *Mutual Aid,* the title of a collection of Kropotkin's essays first published in 1903, envisions anarchism as a mutually-beneficial system of cooperation and reciprocity, whereby the limited success of the competitive struggle between individuals is far outweighed by the collective success of the group in its shared struggle for survival. Historically, these systems have been appropriated by an 'assertive minority' to serve 'its own purposes and create a regime of authority' which, in turn, must 'provoke a reaction among the dispossessed majority' (Miller 1984: 73). Anarchism is, thus, intrinsically a politics of social revolution, as it aims to subdue emerging systems of power, property relations and economic hegemonies. As David Miller suggests, the freedom valued by Kropotkin and, later, the Spanish anarchists, 'is not the freedom of the wilful individualist who turns his back on his social obligations, but the freedom which manifests itself in social solidarity' and the practice of mutual aid (ibid: 160). Like Orwell's own politics, anarchism depends upon the principles of common decency: brotherhood, fair play and honest dealing.

Orwell's critics and biographers often interpret his association with anarchism as exaggeration or misattribution. Robert Benewick and Philip Green, for example, suggest that Orwell's early identification as a 'Tory-anarchist' (cited in Wilkin 2013: 197, n1) was less an affirmation of political allegiance than an effort 'to resist being too easily pigeonholed into an orthodox left of which he was, at best, extremely wary' (Wilkin 2013: 197).[2] John Rodden notes that 'the early announcements that Orwell had "turned anarchist" were all made by critics outside of the anarchist fold and without any intention of "claiming" him' (Rodden 2017: 156). Even George Woodcock opined in his 1946 essay on 'George Orwell, the 19th century liberal' that he lacked 'a deeper understanding' of the politics in which he engaged' (Woodcock 1946: 386), an opinion that suggests Orwell's criticism of anarchism in 'Politics vs. literature – An examination of *Gulliver's Travels*' – in which he asserts that there is a 'totalitarian tendency ... implicit in the anarchist ... vision of Society' (Orwell 2002 [1946c]: 1099) – merely indicated that Orwell was not sufficiently versed in anarchist theory or practice. However, Peter Davison's index of Orwell's pamphlet collection indicates that he had copies of Kropotkin's essay on 'Revolutionary government' (1941) among a variety of other works filed under 'Anarchism: History & Theory' (Davison 2001: 510), so it seems he was familiar enough with the subject to have formulated the opinion expressed in 'The writer's dilemma' – his own review of Woodcock's *The Writer and Politics* – that Kropotkin's 'inventive and pragmatic outlook' made him 'one of the most persuasive of anarchist writers' (Orwell 1948: 3).

Peter Wilkin, on the other hand, takes Orwell at his word and examines what, exactly, the politics of a self-proclaimed Tory-anarchist looks like; he concludes that it 'is not a political ideology

PAPER

in the sense of being a coherent system of principles and beliefs along with ideas about the nature of political power, justice and the basis for a good society. Rather, it is a conservative moral and cultural critique of the modern world that is embodied in the practices and stances of its practitioners' (Wilkin 2013: 198). For Wilkin, this includes:

> ... the use of satire as a means of expressing their cultural and moral opposition to aspects of modernity; often an artistic ambition that surpasses all other motivations; the respect for privacy and the liberty of the individual; a fear of the state and its expanding power over social life; a nostalgic and melancholy temper that laments the passing of an 'Old England'; criticism of social conformism; and a pervasive sense of pessimism about the fate of the modern world (ibid: 199).

While he certainly embodied each of these traits at various points in his political life, the uncharacteristic affection evident in his memory of the Italian militiaman suggests that Orwell's anarchist sympathies run deeper than the nostalgia, fear and pessimism with which Wilkin and others associate them.

THE CONQUEST OF BREAD

While it would be an overstatement to assert that Orwell shared Kropotkin's revolutionary optimism, Orwell would at least agree with his suggestion: 'If the coming revolution is to be a social revolution, it will be distinguished from all former uprisings not only by its aim, but also by its methods' (Kropotkin 1995 [1892]: 52). In *The Conquest of Bread*, Kropotkin acknowledges the failure of the revolutionary attempts of the past, and suggests that these failures share one 'one common feature ... it was always middle class ideals which prevailed. They discussed various political questions at great length, but forgot to discuss the question of bread' (ibid: 52). As the title of Kropotkin's treatise suggests, in anarchist theory – as in Christian prayer – *bread* is a crucial metonym for common necessity and basic human need; more literally, it is also that which is most stringently controlled by the state during social and economic crises.

In denying people bread, either through rationing or commodification, the state denies access to what Kropotkin argues is one of the most fundamental of human rights; as such, its provision must be made central to any revolutionary cause. Kropotkin insists: 'Bread must be found for the people of the revolution, and the question of bread must take precedence ... for in solving the question of bread we must accept the principle of equality, which will force itself upon us to the exclusion of every other solution' (ibid: 55). By stabilising people's tenuous access to bread, the revolution will release them from compulsory indenture to the state; as Kropotkin writes: 'If all the men and women in the countryside had their daily bread assured, and their daily needs already satisfied, who would work for our capitalist?' (ibid: 44). Such were the efforts of the Spanish anarchists to collectivise property, agriculture and industry: without the institutions and authority to control the production and distribution of bread, the capitalist state collapses and the revolution succeeds.

Kropotkin's revolutionary vision is contingent upon the principles of common decency and mutual aid, manifested in the collectivised control and distribution of bread. Though Orwell does not make this theme as explicit as Kropotkin, bread is a similarly persistent concern in *Homage to Catalonia*. He admires, for example, the clever recruit who:

> ... instead of shouting revolutionary slogans ... simply told the Fascists how much better we were fed than they were. His account of the Government rations was apt to be a little imaginative. 'Buttered toast!' – you could hear his voice echoing across the lonely valley – 'We're just sitting down to buttered toast over here!' ... I do not doubt that, like the rest of us, he had not seen [it] for weeks or months past, but in the icy night the news of buttered toast probably set many a Fascist mouth watering. It even made mine water, though I knew he was lying (Orwell 2001 [1938]: 61-62).

Orwell periodically notes the strict rationing and shortage of bread, and remarks on the agonising length of bread-queues even when other supplies are readily available (ibid: 33). Like Kropotkin, he treats bread as an inalienable human right, and is galled by its scarcity among the working classes while the bourgeoisie indulged in epicurean luxuries. He notes that 'restaurants and hotels seemed to have little difficulty in getting whatever they wanted, but in the working-class quarters the queues for bread, olive oil, and other necessaries were hundreds of yards long' (ibid: 98). For Orwell, the indecency of 'A fat man eating quails while children are begging for bread' (ibid: 100) is tantamount to treason.

Orwell is also critical of the inequitable distribution of bread even amongst his own militia group under the Workers' Party of Marxist Unification (POUM). Orwell enlisted with the POUM immediately upon his arrival in Barcelona, without realising that the organisation was already set up for betrayal by the communists he mistook as allies. Even without this knowledge, Orwell is appalled by his militia's 'frightful wastage of food, especially bread. From my barrack-room alone a basketful of bread was thrown away at every meal – a disgraceful thing when the civilian population was short of it' (ibid: 34). He is similarly disheartened that 'Boys of fifteen were being brought up for enlistment by their parents ... for the sake of the bread which the militia received in plenty and could smuggle home to their parents' (ibid: 38).[3] Though Orwell does not directly state as much, this unequal distribution of bread foreshadowed the fragmentation of the resistance, as it revealed that the anti-fascist cause was not the united front he initially perceived.

COMMUNIST BETRAYAL

At this time, the left was composed of three major organisations: the Unified Socialist Party of Catalonia, or PSUC (*Partit Socialista Unificat de Catalunya*), a fusion of Marxist parties under communist control; the Workers' Party of Marxist Unification, or POUM (*Partido Obrero de Unificación Marxista*), the anti-Stalinist militia group to which Orwell belonged, and the anarchist revolutionaries of the CNT-FAI, the National Confederation of Labour (*Confederación Nacional del Trabajo*) and Iberian Anarchist Federation (*Federación Anarquista Ibérica*). Orwell confesses in his memoir that at the time he enlisted:

> I did not realize that there were differences between the political parties. … I thought it was idiotic that people fighting for their lives should *have* separate parties; my attitude was always, 'Why can't we drop all this political nonsense and get on with the war?' This was, of course, the correct 'anti-Fascist' attitude which had been carefully disseminated by the English newspapers, largely in order to prevent people from grasping the real nature of the struggle (ibid: 170).[4]

Though the three groups were superficially united under the anti-fascist Republican cause, their goals were significantly divergent. Orwell summarises their positions as follows: 'On the one side [was] the CNT-FAI, the POUM, and a section of the Socialists, standing for workers' control: on the other side [was] the Right-wing Socialists, Liberals, and Communists, standing for centralized government and a militarized army' (ibid: 182). As Orwell explains, after coming under communist control, the PSUC was, in fact, the least revolutionary of the groups, and the party line propagated by the pro-communist press asserted: 'Whoever tries to turn the civil war into a social revolution is playing into the hands of the Fascists and is in effect, if not in intention, a traitor' (ibid: 180). The POUM, conversely, argued that the 'war and the revolution are inseparable. … If the workers do not control the armed forces, the armed forces will control the workers' (ibid: 181). The POUM was, thus, more closely allied with the CNT-FAI in their advocacy of workers' control and support for the revolution.

However, the CNT-FAI differed fundamentally from the other two organisations because, as Orwell asserts, the 'Communist's emphasis is always on centralism and efficiency, [while] the Anarchist's [is] on liberty and equality' (ibid: 182). The CNT-FAI distinguished themselves from the communist organisations in their opposition to parliamentary democracy, and their commitment to restoring power and control to the workers through social revolution (Orwell

1938: 181). Orwell describes the persistence of the 'revolutionary spirit' on the anarchist-controlled Aragón front, recalling that:

> General and private, peasant and militiaman, still met as equals; everyone drew the same pay, wore the same clothes, ate the same food and called everyone else 'thou' and 'comrade'; there was no boss-class, no menial-class, no beggars, no prostitutes, no lawyers, no priests, no boot-licking, no cap-touching. I was breathing the air of equality, and I was simple enough to imagine that it existed all over Spain. I did not realise that more or less by chance I was isolated among the most revolutionary section of the Spanish working class (ibid: 186).

The egalitarian camaraderie Orwell and the POUM shared with the anarchists in Aragón was not replicated in areas of other Spain, particularly not those under communist control.

The fragmentation of the Left began towards the end of 1936, when power shifted hands from the anarchists to the communists, who had begun working actively against any revolutionary efforts (ibid: 101). Though the PSUC, POUM and CNT-FAI were ideologically united in their collective fight against fascism, the communist forces endeavoured to suppress the revolution and, by extension, the organisations that supported it. The loss of the battle of Málaga in early 1937 signified for Orwell his first sense of uncertainty about the solidarity of the left. He and 'every man in the militia believed that the loss of Málaga was due to treachery. It was the first talk I had heard of treachery or divided aims. It set up in my mind the first vague doubt about this war in which, hitherto, the rights and wrongs had seemed so beautifully simple' (ibid: 63). Later, on the Aragón front, Orwell had 'very little doubt that arms were deliberately withheld' by the Communists, 'lest too may of them should get into the hands of the Anarchists, who would afterwards use them for revolutionary purposes' (ibid: 187).[5] Ultimately, it was the attack on the Telephone Exchange and subsequent riots in Barcelona in May 1937 that brought to a head the antagonisms between the communist and anarchist forces, and contributed to the widespread feeling that 'the revolution had been sabotaged' (ibid: 191). Orwell recalls that there 'was a general impression that the [Republican] Assault Guards were "after" the CNT and the working class' (ibid: 191), and as a result, the revolutionaries now faced two enemies: the fascists *and* the communists.

The communists' sedition strengthened the POUM's solidarity with the CNT; as Orwell notes, their tactics drove the two parties together. 'When the POUM joined in the disastrous fighting in Barcelona in May, it was mainly from instinct to stand by the CNT, and later, when the POUM was suppressed, the Anarchists were the only people who dared to raise a voice in its defence' (ibid: 182). The POUM and the CNT became scapegoats for the communists, who claimed

DANA WIGHT

the May riots were part of an anarchist plot to sabotage the left, and that the revolutionaries were actually in fascist pay. They were denounced as traitors and Trotskyists, and the communists began imprisoning anyone associated with the anarchists. In the midst of the riots, Orwell witnessed the treachery first-hand as Republican Assault Guards attacked the revolutionaries, and he recalls in his memoir the moment when his allegiances became clear: 'On one side [was] the CNT, on the other side the police … when I see an actual flesh-and-blood worker in conflict with his natural enemy, the policeman, I do not have to ask myself which side I am on' (ibid: 106). The communist betrayal of the anarchists was, for Orwell, a more personal betrayal of his own politics of brotherhood, fair play and honest dealing.

DEFENCE OF THE SPANISH ANARCHISTS

The POUM and the Spanish anarchists were vilified not only by the PSUC and communist sympathisers in Spain, but also the European press and left-leaning intelligentsia abroad. In his 1946 essay 'Why I write,' Orwell maintains that his writing is motivated by 'a feeling of partisanship, a sense of injustice … because there is some lie that I want to expose, some fact to which I want to draw attention' (Orwell 2001 [1946b]: 462). In the case of *Homage to Catalonia*, this sense of injustice emanates from the English misrepresentation and communist persecution of the anarchists during the Spanish civil war. *Homage to Catalonia* is, thus, more than a memoir; it is also an effort on Orwell's part to hold the communists accountable for the loss of the war and to vindicate the anarchists in the eyes of the English left. He asserts that 'it was the Communists above all others who prevented revolution in Spain' (Orwell 2001 [1938]: 178) – a betrayal that was, in part, abetted by communist sympathisers in England and by the European press.

Among the many things Orwell disapproved of in the popular press was its treatment of the anarchists, who were consistently misrepresented. He suggests that accounts of the revolutionary efforts were suppressed outside of Spain because 'every English-speaking person shudders at the name of "Anarchist"' (ibid: 201) and laments that 'it is almost impossible to get anyone to print anything in their defence' (ibid: 198) – an exclusion that seems to have prompted Orwell to set the record straight in his own accounts of the war. In his review of Mairin Mitchell's *Storm Over Spain* (1937), for example, Orwell expresses frustration over the popular assumption that 'Anarchism is the same thing as anarchy' while lauding 'what Spanish Anarchism stands for, and the remarkable things it achieved' (Orwell 2001 [1937b]: 257). He also chides Robert Sencourt, author of *Spain's Ordeal* (1937), for using the term '"Anarchism" indifferently with "anarchy," which is hardly more correct use of the words than saying that a Conservative is one who makes jam' (Orwell 2001 [1937c]: 298). Perhaps most damningly, in his essay 'Spilling the Spanish Beans', Orwell is alarmed by the English people's failure to identify communism as 'a counter-revolutionary force' and asserts that 'Communists everywhere are in alliance with bourgeois reformism and using the whole of their powerful machinery to crush or discredit any party that shows signs of revolutionary tendencies' (Orwell 2001 [1937a]: 216). Wilkin theorises that Orwell was 'perpetually distrustful of the socialism to which he was instinctively drawn ... because he feared that in practice it would be led and dominated by intellectuals and the middle classes, not the working classes, and the former would adopt the authoritarian means to bring about the progress they desired' (Wilkin 2013: 200). The communists' betrayal of the Spanish anarchists and their revolutionary cause solidified this fear, and in addition to the Spanish 'Beans', Orwell spilled considerable ink in support of the anarchists following the war.

Orwell indignantly refused to participate in the intellectual debates concerning the war following his return to England in July 1937. When solicited on behalf of the *Left Review* to contribute to a pamphlet of contemporary authors' takes on the Spanish war, Orwell emphatically declined, asserting that 'Fascism is being riveted on the Spanish workers under the pretext of resisting Fascism,' and denouncing the journal's solicitation as pandering to the politically-inept 'fashionable pansies' of the English literati (Orwell 2001 [1937d]: 249). To the solicitor, he writes: 'No doubt you know something about the inner history of the war and have deliberately joined in the defence of "democracy" (i.e. capitalism) racket in order to aid in the crushing of the Spanish working class and thus indirectly defend your dirty little dividends' (ibid: 249-250). Unsurprisingly, his contribution was not published. Nor was the letter Orwell sent to the *Daily Herald* and the *New Statesman & Nation*, in which he sought to defend the legal rights of former POUM members being tried for espionage (Orwell 2001 [1938]).[6] In the letter, Orwell points toward the dubious nature of the evidence against them, and suggests that the 'prosecution is taking place not at the will of the Spanish Government but in response to outside pressure as a part of the world-wide campaign against "Trotskyism"' (ibid: 306). For Orwell, this campaign and its persistent mis-association of the POUM and anarchist revolutionaries with Trotskyism was a direct result of the communist betrayal of the Spanish working class, the misrepresentation of their revolutionary efforts in the European press, and the political inertia of the left-leaning English intelligentsia.

Orwell's frustration with English armchair socialism continued into the early years of the Second World War, during which time he vacillated in his own political identifications but remained steadfastly committed to anti-fascist action and critical of working class complacency. In a letter to the *Partisan Review*, Orwell states

PAPER

that 'the belief in international working class solidarity doesn't exist any longer'; he blames this disillusion on the 'utter failure of the European working class to stand together in the face of Fascist regression' (Orwell 2001 [1941a]: 341-342). Orwell excoriates the docility of the European workers who 'failed to stage even a single strike in aid of their Spanish comrades,' seemingly because 'it was virtually impossible to get them to see that what happened in Spain concerned them in any way' (ibid: 342). He turns on his own brief pre-war pacifism[7] to denounce 'all the English left-wingers' who proclaimed to be '"anti-Fascist" but in a purely negative way – "against" Fascism without being "for" any discoverable policy – [as] underneath it lay the flabby idea that when the time came the Russians would do our fighting for us' (Orwell 2001 [1941b]: 131). Or course, by September 1941, the fascist threat to the working class had spread significantly, and the Germans occupied large swathes of Russian industrial zones. Orwell laments:

> If even the shadow of international working class solidarity existed, Stalin would only have to call on the German workers in the name of the Socialist Fatherland for the German war-effort to be sabotaged ... but the Russians do not even issue any such appeal. They know it is useless ... At present the world is atomised and no form of internationalism has any power or even much appeal. This may be painful to literary circles in Cambridge, but it is the fact (Orwell 2001 [1941a]: 342).

For Orwell, the failure of the European working class to unite against fascism – first during the Spanish war, and again as Germany marched over Russia – signified the death of the 'earthly paradise' of the socialist revolutionary cause.

In his notes commemorating the eighth anniversary of the start of the Spanish civil war, Orwell describes the conflict as the 'curtain-raiser of the present struggle and one of the most tragic as well as one of the most sordid events that modern Europe has seen' (Orwell 2001 [1944]: 367). As the true scope of the horrors of the Holocaust would not emerge for several years, Orwell could not have known how tragic and sordid modern European history would become; however, his admonishment of British non-intervention in the Spanish war anticipates the culpability of the Allied nations in both Franco's and Hitler's successes. He writes: 'The story is a disgusting one, because of the sordid behaviour of the Great Powers and the indifference of the world at large ... The British and French simply looked the other way while their enemies triumphed and their friends were destroyed. The British attitude is the hardest to forgive, because it was foolish as well as dishonourable' (ibid: 368-369). The inaction of the European powers, and of Britain in particular, during the Spanish civil war betrayed not only the Spanish working class, but Orwell's own principles of brotherhood, fair play, and honest dealing, which, to his mind, enabled the rise of fascism across Europe.

Perhaps Orwell's persistent sense of betrayal – by the communists in Spain, by the Great European Powers, and by the soft socialism of the English left – contributed to the compilation of his list of 'crypto-communists and fellow-travellers,' submitted to the British Information Research Department in 1949 (Orwell 2001 [1949]). His experiences in Spain made him wary of the potential for communist treachery and its totalitarian tendencies, and he held fast to the conviction that they had cost the Spanish working class their revolution. As David Goodway notes, in the final decade of his life Orwell 'was a left-wing socialist and supporter of the Labour Party; yet at the same time he exhibited pronounced anarchist tendencies and sympathies' (Goodway 2016: 48). Even when Orwell was critical of anarchist ideology (and, as a rule, Orwell was critical of ideology in general), he staunchly defended the Spanish anarchists and their revolutionary efforts until his death in January 1950. As Bernard Crick suggests: 'He did not accept anarchism in principle, but had, as a socialist who distrusted any kind of state power, a speculative and personal sympathy with anarchists' (Crick 1980: 308). Orwell's anarchism was, thus, perhaps less of an ideological allegiance than an empathetic fraternity with the Spanish anarchists – an emotional as well as political affinity with a working class who, against considerable odds, spent two and a half years fighting against organised fascism and its enablers in an effort to realise the socialist vision Orwell shared.

CONCLUSION

Orwell's enduring respect for the Spanish anarchists is reflected not only in his vehement defence of their actions and principles, but also in his resolute belief in the integrity of their struggle. For Orwell, the revolutionary spirit of the Spanish working-class is indicative of a purpose higher than that of resistance to fascism 'in the name of "democracy" and the *status quo*,' as it was 'the kind of effort that could probably only be made by people who were fighting with a revolutionary intention – [who] believed that they were fighting for something better than the *status quo*' (Orwell 2001 [1938a]: 171). The immediate solidarity Orwell feels with the Italian militiaman and the principles for which he stands is extended to the Spanish revolutionary cause as a whole – something Orwell recognised immediately as 'a state of affairs worth fighting for' (ibid: 33). He reflects: 'Above all, there was a belief in the revolution and the future, a feeling of having suddenly emerged into an era of equality and freedom. Human beings were trying to behave as human beings and not as cogs in the capitalist machine' (ibid: 33). The righteous conviction with which Orwell imbues his descriptions of the revolutionary cause seems largely an effect of the anarchists' 'crystal spirit'.

It is this spirit that distinguishes Orwell's own nebulous politics from the various factions that have and continue to attempt to claim him as their own. He notes that the effect of his experiences in Spain 'was to make my desire to see Socialism established much more actual than it had been before' (Orwell 2001 [1938a]: 91) because his socialist vision had been achieved, at least for a time, by the Spanish anarchists. He writes:

> One had been in a community where hope was more normal than apathy or cynicism, where the word 'comrade' stood for comradeship and not, as in most countries, for humbug. One had breathed the air of equality. I am well aware that it is now the fashion to deny that Socialism has anything to do with equality. In every country in the world a huge tribe of party-hacks and sleek little professors are busing 'proving' that Socialism means no more than a planned state-capitalism with the grab-motive left intact. But fortunately there also exists a vision of Socialism quite different from this. The thing that attracts ordinary men to Socialism and makes them willing to risk their skins for it … is the idea of equality; to the vast majority of people Socialism means a classless society, or nothing at all (ibid: 91).

Because, as George Woodcock acknowledged, Orwell 'was never in any sense a party man' (Woodcock 1966: 56), he does not hesitate to denounce the shortcomings or inconsistencies of even those political positions with which he is sympathetic. He distances himself from the so-called socialist 'party-hacks' and the counter-revolutionary communists and allies himself in spirit, if not in name, with an anarchist vision of society in which one's 'daily bread' is produced and distributed by and for the workers, basic human needs are satisfied through systems of mutual aid, and the principles of common decency are upheld. Orwell reflects that the months he spent in the Spanish militias were invaluable to him because they were a microcosm of a classless society, and they demonstrated, at least temporarily, that such a society was possible (ibid: 91).

NOTES

[1] Orwell's own definition of socialism shares Kropotkin's fundamental principles, namely that the 'basis of Socialism is humanism' (Orwell 2001 [1946b]: 422): 'Underneath it lies the belief that human nature is fairly decent to start with and is capable of indefinite development' (ibid: 424)

[2] Though Orwell had long since abandoned the identity himself, in his 1946 examination of *Gulliver's Travels*, he describes Jonathan Swift as a 'Tory anarchist': one who despises 'authority while disbelieving in liberty, and preserving the aristocratic outlook while seeing clearly that the existing aristocracy is degenerate and contemptible' (Orwell 2002 [1946c]: 1100)

[3] Orwell reflects that a number of POUM recruits had enlisted 'for the sake of a job. The fact that in December 1936 there was already a serious bread shortage in Barcelona and militiamen got bread in plenty had a lot to do with this' (Orwell 2001 [c1939]: 286)

[4] Later, in his 'Notes on the Spanish Militias' (c1939), Orwell asserts that the differences between the parties 'had been covered up in the English leftwing press'; in hindsight, he acknowledges that 'Had I had a complete understanding of the situation I should probably have joined the CNT militia' (Orwell 2001 [c1939]: 278)

[5] Orwell later notes that the accusations of arms-treachery largely consisted of 'vague rumours that "they," usually meaning the PSUC, had stolen guns etc. meant for ourselves' (Orwell 2001 [c1939]: 284). Following the Huesca attack in June 1937, however, it became clear to Orwell through the first-hand accounts of those who fought that the Republicans 'deliberately withheld the artillery to get as many POUM troops killed as possible' (ibid: 289)

[6] The letter was ultimately published by the *Manchester Guardian* on 5 August 1938. The *New Statesman & Nation* confirmed receipt of the letter but declined to print it; the *Daily Herald* did not acknowledge its submission (Orwell 2001 [1938]: 305)

[7] In a letter to the editor of the *New English Weekly*, Orwell succinctly describes his pacifist position as deriving from the 'truth … that any real [social] advance, let alone any genuinely revolutionary change, can only begin then the mass of the people definitely refuse capitalist-imperialist war" (Orwell 2001 [1938c]: 30)

REFERENCES

Crick, Bernard (1980) *George Orwell: A Life*, London: Secker & Warburg

Davison, Peter (ed.) (2001) Extracts from Orwell's pamphlet collection catalogue, *Orwell and Politics*, New York: Penguin pp 509-512

Feaver, George (1994) Orwell, Woodcock, and St. George, Symposium on the Achievement of George Woodcock, Vancouver, Canada: University of British Columbia, May

Goodway, David (2016) Orwell and anarchism, *George Orwell Studies*, Vol. 1, No. 1 pp 37-55

Kropotkin, Peter (1895 [1887]) *Anarchist Communism: Its Basis and Principles*, London: Freedom Office, second edition

Kropotkin, Peter (1995 [1892]) *The Conquest of Bread and Other Writings*, Shatz, Marshall S. (ed.) Cambridge: Cambridge University Press

Kropotkin, Peter (1989 [1902]) *Mutual Aid*, Montréal, Canada: Black Rose

Miller, David (1984) *Anarchism*, London: Dent

Orwell, George (2001 [1937a]) Spilling the Spanish beans, Davison, Peter (ed.) *Orwell in Spain*, New York: Penguin pp 215-223

Orwell, George (2001 [1937b]) Review of *Storm Over Spain*, by Mairin Mitchell, Davison, Peter (ed.) *Orwell in Spain*, New York: Penguin pp 257-259

Orwell, George (2001 [1937c]) Review of *Spain's Ordeal*, by Robert Sencourt, 23 June, *New English Weekly*, Davison, Peter (ed.) *Orwell in Spain*, New York: Penguin pp 297-299

Orwell, George (2001 [1937d]) Unpublished response to *Authors Take Sides on the Spanish War*, Davison, Peter (ed.) *Orwell in Spain*, New York: Penguin pp 248-250

Orwell, George (2001 [1938a]) *Homage to Catalonia*, Davison, Peter (ed.) *Orwell in Spain*, New York: Penguin pp 31-215

Orwell, George (2001 [1938b]) To the editor, *Manchester Guardian*, Davison, Peter (ed.) *Orwell in Spain*, New York: Penguin pp 305-308

Orwell, George (2001 [1938c]) To the editor, *New English Weekly*, Davison, Peter (ed.) *Orwell and Politics*, New York: Penguin pp 28-31

Orwell, George (2001 [c1939]) Notes on the Spanish militias, Davison, Peter (ed.) *Orwell in Spain*, New York: Penguin pp 277-289

Orwell, George (2001 [1941a]) Extract from letter to *Partisan Review*, Davison, Peter (ed.) *Orwell in Spain*, New York: Penguin pp 341-342

Orwell, George (2001 [1941b]) The lion and the unicorn: Socialism and the English genius, Davison, Peter (ed.) *Orwell and Politics*, New York: Penguin pp 103-139

Orwell, George (2001 [1943]) Looking back on the Spanish War, Davison, Peter (ed.) *Orwell in Spain*, New York: Penguin pp 343-364

Orwell, George (2001 [1944]) The eight years of war: Spanish memories, Davison, Peter (ed.) *Orwell in Spain*, New York: Penguin pp 367-369

Orwell, George (2001 [1946a]) What is Socialism?, Davison, Peter (ed.) *Orwell and Politics*, New York: Penguin pp 420-425

Orwell, George (2001 [1946b]) Why I write, Davison, Peter (ed.) *Orwell and Politics*, New York: Penguin pp 457-464

Orwell, George (2002 [1946c]) Politics vs. literature – An examination of *Gulliver's Travels*, Carey, John (ed.) *Essays*, New York: Knopf pp 1088-1108

Orwell, George (1948) The writer's dilemma [review of *The Writer and Politics* by George Woodcock], *Observer*, 22 August p. 3

Orwell, George (2001 [1949]) Extracts from Orwell's list of crypto-communists and fellow travellers, Davison, Peter (ed.) *Orwell and Politics*, New York: Penguin pp 501-509

Rodden, John (2017) *The Politics of Literary Reputation*, Abingdon, Oxon: Routledge

Wilkin, Peter (2013) George Orwell: The English dissident as Tory anarchist, *Political Studies*, Vol. 16 pp 197-214

Woodcock, George (1946) George Orwell, 19th century liberal, *Politics*, December pp 384-388

Woodcock, George (1966) *The Crystal Spirit*, Boston: Little, Brown

NOTE ON THE CONTRIBUTOR

Dana Wight (PhD, University of Alberta) is an English instructor at NorQuest College in Edmonton, Alberta, Canada, where she is also Vice-Chair of the NorQuest College Research Ethics Board. Her research interests and academic publications include work in feminist psychoanalytic theory, gothic literature and the British novel. She also hosts a community radio programme featuring music inspired by literature: episode 14 is dedicated to George Orwell's *Nineteen Eighty-Four*.

PAPER

Surveillance From Orwell to *Orwell*: The Power of Vision in Popular Culture

XIAOZHOU LI

In Nineteen Eighty-Four *(1949), Orwell pictures a powerful force of totalitarian surveillance that watches, deters and controls. The idea of surveillance has been a popular theme inspired by* Nineteen Eighty-Four *and explored by popular culture. This paper focuses on the presentation and reflection of surveillance in Orwell's dystopian masterpiece as well as novels and videogames inspired by it. In* 1985 *(1983) by György Dalos and* 1Q84 *(2009-2010) by Haruki Murakami, the authors explore possible changes and variations based on or borrowing an Orwellian imagination of surveillance. Videogames, on the other hand, approach the idea of surveillance in a more immersive and experimental way. In* Papers, Please *(2013),* Beholder *(2016),* Replica *(2016) and* Orwell: Keeping an Eye On You *(2016), the player – whether inside the screen as a virtual participant of the event or beyond the game in reality as an experiencer – becomes both the subject and the object, both the executor and the victim of surveillance.*

Keywords: *Nineteen Eighty-Four*, surveillance, totalitarianism, inspired work, videogame

THE VISION OF POWER AND THE POWER OF VISION

George Orwell's dystopian novel *Nineteen Eighty-Four* (1949) features a world under the constant surveillance of telescreens – 'BIG BROTHER IS WATCHING YOU' is written everywhere. It resonates in modern readers' minds with the famous opening of the 2011 CBS sci-fi crime drama, *Person of Interest*: 'You are being watched. The government has a secret system. … A Machine that spies on you every hour of every day.' In the drama, a surveillance AI provides the social security numbers of prospective victims for a vigilante group of former agents to trace and save lives. Yet the surveillance in *PoI* and in *Nineteen Eighty-Four* are not only different in purpose but also different in method. *PoI* portrays a spectacle of 'new surveillance' defined by Gary Marx (2007: 88-89) as formed of multimedia, with cutting-edge technology; intensive, invisible and intangible. *Nineteen Eighty-Four* stays in the 'traditional surveillance' mode. Unlike new surveillance, it focuses more on personal behaviour and less on personal information. If the Machine in *PoI* uncovers the villains by gathering their location, personal history, interpersonal relationships and even personalities to infer the crime yet to be committed, then the telescreens and Secret Police uncover the 'villains' by observing anyone at any time and revealing those committing the 'crime'.

Whether traditional or new, the fundamental structure of surveillance is a simple bilateral relationship: someone is watching and someone is being watched. The objectification of the 'object' of surveillance inherently happens under the inequality and imbalance of power. Moreover, if the object can be watched, it can reasonably be heard, touched, or understood. In addition, the self-authorised power of looking symbolises the potential of omniscience and thus omnipotence. As Neil Richards points out, surveillance endows the watcher with the potential ability of 'sinisterness' since it 'distorts the power relationships between the watcher and the watched, enhancing the watcher's ability to blackmail, coerce and discriminate against the people under its scrutiny' (2013: 1936).

There are two classic models of panoptic surveillance: Benthamian, in *Panopticon* (1791), and Foucauldian, in *Discipline and Punish* (1975). In Bentham's panoptic prison, each prisoner stays in an individual cell in an annular building surrounding a central tower. Panoptic surveillance provides 'uninterrupted exposure [of prisoners] to invisible inspection' (Bentham 1843 [1791]: 86) and enables the guards to surveil in secret. Yet Foucault further develops the model, in which surveillance works visibly, to make the prisoner aware of being 'seen, but he does not see; he is the object of information, never a subject in communication' (Foucault 1991 [1975]: 200). As Elmer summarises, what distinguishes Foucauldian surveillance from Benthamian surveillance is its 'perspective', as for the former 'the prisoners, not the tower, are at the centre of the panopticon' (2012: 22). In a Foucauldian panopticon, the play of visibility is transferred into the play of power. On the one hand, surveillance becomes 'an important mechanism, for it automatises and disindivisualises power'; instead of imposing on individuals, power is executed by 'a certain concerted distribution' to 'produce the relation in which individuals are caught up' (Foucault 1991 [1975]: 202). On the other hand, Foucauldian surveillance, whose core is 'disciplinary control' (Lianos 2010: 70), works in the form of self-surveillance. The power of the watcher and the power of the watched are unequal: the former can see and control the latter, while the latter cannot interfere in surveillance. Therefore, once aware of the existence of a watcher, the watched have to suppose the constant presence of it in order to behave themselves and avoid punishment. They are in practice under self-surveillance and become the *de facto* watcher.

This is the trick Orwell plays on Winston Smith in *Nineteen Eighty-Four*. It is a world of Foucauldian surveillance (Booker 1994: 79) that desires and seizes power, with citizens always watched openly and encouraged to watch others. When a citizen looks at the face of Big Brother on the telescreen, Big Brother is also watching them. '6079 Smith W.! Yes, *you*! Bend lower, please!' (Orwell 1954 [1949]: 32). When Smith struggles to bend his back during the physical Jerks, the telescreen barks at him. It directly, and almost proudly, reminds every member of the society of their visibility. 'There was of course no way of knowing whether you were being watched at any given moment. ... You had to live – did live, from habit that became instinct – in the assumption that every sound you made was overheard, and, except in darkness, every movement scrutinised' (ibid: 6). Yet, surveillance in *Nineteen Eighty-Four* is a mixture of Benthamian and Foucauldian. Yeo (2010: 53-55) believes that Smith's vain expectation of a secret corner to breathe in a Foucauldian panopticon leads to his arrest, but he fails to grasp the root of this fatal mistake. The arrest of Smith in his secret nest, as well as his vain expectation, results from his neglect of the Benthamian possibility of his surveillance. He takes it for granted that the surveillance is all Foucauldian, since as long as he watches Big Brother, he knows Big Brother is watching him. He fails to realise that Big Brother also observes in a Benthamian way; when he does not watch Big Brother, Big Brother is still watching him.

Meanwhile, the Party's stress on informing, confessing or 'selling' (as sung in the nursery rhyme about the 'spreading chestnut tree') (Orwell 1954 [1949]: 64), encourages people to lose faith in each other, even in the most intimate families. Like the panoptic prison, it divides *people* into many *persons*. At the beginning of the novel Smith is struck by 'the look of helpless fright on [Mrs. Parsons'] greyish face' in front of her children (ibid: 22), but he comes to understand that the children are 'taught to spy on them and report their deviations. ... It was a device by means of which everyone could be surrounded night and day by informers who knew him intimately' (ibid: 109). Failing to trust means the elimination of safety, as anyone can be a reporter, and no place is a safe house. One is completely isolated; everyone watches and watches out for others. 'Proles and animals are free' (ibid: 60), because they are not objectifying and objectified under surveillance. When people watch not only themselves but also others around them, they become in practice accomplices of the Big Brother totalitarianism. It is an easy mistake to make. Arendt names it 'the banality of evil' (2006, cited in Williams 2017: 21); Freedman names it 'the breakdown of common sense' (1984: 615); Gottlieb calls it 'organised injustice' (2011: 30), as 'the individual has become a victim, experiencing loss of control over his or her destiny in the face of a monstrous, suprahuman force' (ibid: 11); and Spender highlights man's use of 'machinery in order to condition his own consciousness' (1971: 66). The quicksand of self-surveillance traps all.

XIAOZHOU LI THE INSPIRATION FROM *NINETEEN EIGHTY-FOUR* AND THE DEVELOPMENT OF SURVEILLANCE

Nineteen Eighty-Four has had enduring inspiration in all fields of popular art and culture. The work itself has been adapted into stage performances (e.g. an opera by Lorin Maazel 2005, a play by Robert Icke and Duncan Macmillan 2013, and ballet by Northern Ballet in 2016), television and radio programmes (many produced by the BBC), and films, the latest directed by Paul Greengrass due to be released in 2019. Many novels, comics and songs employ its symbolic elements. In more recent years, videogame developers have also been attracted to the idea of dystopian society, surveillance and the Thought Police. These works, however, do not necessarily follow the original design and intention of *Nineteen Eighty-Four*. They may discuss more advanced forms and techniques of surveillance, or depict what has happened instead of suggesting what could happen. Just as Orwell injected his own understanding and expectation of the era,[1] so do authors and designers in the modern day.

'The best thing that could happen to George Orwell is unquestionably 1985,' claims Sandison (1986: 191). '[All] apocalypses, in the literary sense, are failed apocalypses,' according to Bloom (1987: 3). The writings of György Dalos, however, may raise questions about these two points. His *1985* (1981), a sequel to *Nineteen Eighty-Four*, portrays an eventful year full of political turbulence and dramatic changes in Oceania in the form of a historical report beginning with the death of Big Brother. During the jostling for power between two political factions, O'Brien and his Thought Police are forced to stand neutral and ironically play the role of 'the defender of freedom of thought' (Dalos 1983 [1981]: 27). He sets up the *Times Literary Supplement*, recruiting Smith, Julia, Parsons, and Syme as editors. When thoughts are gradually liberated, the totalitarian government gradually loses control of its emancipated people. A revolution breaks out but fails. Finally, a new Eurasia-dominated regime is established. Surveillance returns, the leader of revolt is hanged and Smith is sentenced to thirty years' imprisonment.

Central to *1985* are not the models of surveillance but the phases of surveillance. It describes the chaotic yet temporarily free period during the transition of one totalitarian government to another. Dalos explains how the after-effects of surveillance gradually fade, and why the transition of power called back the terror of surveillance. After the death of Big Brother, governmental surveillance gradually loosens and 'the horse has bolted' (ibid: 28). Self-surveillance still exists, but in a different form. On the one hand, as Smith notes, *TLS* editors 'achieved a situation which was previously unimaginable, that we were able to be our own censors' (ibid: 40). Yet, on the other hand, people still 'fight against the heritage of Big Brother' (ibid: 43):

Syme's favourite pastime was to scare us continually. One fine day, he prophesied, there would be an official announcement in the *Times* which would claim the whole liberal era was only a joke, that Big Brother was not dead but only wanted to check in this way how many loyal supporters he still had in Oceania – and who the traitors were. ... We almost killed ourselves laughing except for Parsons, who found nothing witty in Syme's prophecy and begged him desperately to stop his bad joke (ibid 45-46).

The weakening and eventually interruption of surveillance made people dare to write 'truth for the first time' yet leads to 'the beginning of the end' for Oceania (ibid: 94). As Arendt comments, totalitarianism has 'disregard for facts [and] strict adherence to the rules of a fictitious world' (2017 [1951]). Once the facts are recalled and the fictitious world is exposed, it will soon 'collapse within months or even weeks' due to 'lack of self-confidence' (Dalos 1983 [1981]: 57).

The collapse of the old Oceanian system, in effect, leads to the collapse of totalitarianism in which surveillance is one of the most important and efficient tools to supervise, deter, and thus control. The gradual fading of surveillance not only indicates the fall of the totalitarian system, but also accelerates this process. The establishment of a new system dominated by Eurasia, however, helps restore totalitarianism and so the Big Brother surveillance returns. The rebuilding of surveillance, in a similar way, not only indicates the return of the totalitarian system, but also accelerates it. The Eurasian 'keeping-smile pistol' (ibid: 108) fires if someone does not smile. In front of the pistol, tears 'flowed from some people's eyes while they smiled; others turned round so that, for a few seconds at least, they could make a face that corresponded to their state of mind' (ibid: 108). Facing telescreens, everyone needs to 'dissemble your feelings, to control your face, to do what everyone else was doing, was an instinctive reaction' (Orwell 1954 [1949]: 17). Moreover, even the 'historian' who writes the 'historical report' *1985* is under close surveillance. There is 'an egg-shaped apparatus the size of a hand' hiding in their office, eavesdropping on their work (Dalos 1983 [1981]: 95, n79). All this suggests that the freedom of Oceania with the new government is merely an illusion, as surveillance and its control will never end as long as the system of totalitarianism lasts. Big Brother died, and 'Little Brother' became the new leader (ibid: 107, n83).

As Booker argues, the 'satire of Dalos's book is directed not only at the structures of official power ... but also at the opponents of such power and at their tendency either to be ineffectual or to be conscripted into the service of official power' (op cit: 114). Dalos, unlike Orwell, intends his novel to be a criticism of an authentic past instead of a warning about a possible future.[2] He wishes the readers to bring in their own history when reading the book and to bear in mind that 'all of us play – can play – a role in the world history' in the preface to the Chinese translation (2011: 1, my translation). *1985* attempts to 'inherit the intelligent legacy of Orwell's, and to tell the authentic life of East-European people in [Dalos's] own language' (ibid: 158, my translation). So this incorporates not only the fate of the country but also his personal experience: the governmental accusation of being Maoist, the police surveillance and the prohibition of his books for around twenty years (ibid: 1). When the novel 'was finally published in Hungary in 1990, people were astounded by the author's foresight', commented Yu, the Chinese translator of *1985*. 'But of course, rather than "foresight", I would give credit to Dalos thorough understanding the logic of totalitarianism' (ibid: 159, my translation).

If *1985* focuses more on the phases of surveillance, then *1Q84* (Murakami 2009-2010) investigates a more modern form of surveillance. In its three books and 925 pages, *1Q84* creates an intricate world, full of specious clues without ends, questions concerning key characters and notions unanswered, and multiple themes: dystopian society, religion and cult, reality and fiction, authority and authorship, good and evil, etc.[3] Many Murakami scholars claim that the connections between *1Q84* and *Nineteen Eighty-Four* are weak and only in the form of wordplay,[4] yet this is a superficial misreading. From one perspective, Murakami has clearly indicated the close relationship between *Nineteen Eighty-Four* and *1Q84*. In fact, the novel was almost named *1985* (Ōi 2009). When interviewed about *1Q84*, he commented: 'For long I have wanted to write a novel about the near past based on George Orwell's futuristic novel *Nineteen Eighty-Four*' (Ozaki 2009). From another perspective, the connection between *Nineteen Eighty-Four* and *1Q84* is not about the superficial similarity of settings, but about the underlying theme of surveillance they both discuss. In its timeline, *1Q84* does not depict George Orwell's near future 'but the opposite – the near past – of 1984' (Murakami 2010). Yet for its structuring of surveillance, it does not show how surveillance may appear in the future but how surveillance appears at present. There is 'no longer any place for a Big Brother' (Murakami 2011: 227), as he infiltrates through the body of 'Little People', who watch over and control only in a more fragmentary, circuitous and invisible way. Little People and Big Brother are two sides of a same coin.

1Q84 tells how Aomame and Tengo, two childhood friends who have lost contact with each other, reunite in 'another' reality. The year of *1Q84* is a parallel to the reality of *Nineteen Eighty-Four* and a world with two moons. Accidentally breaking into *1Q84*, Aomame is an instructor at a deluxe sports club and also a killer hired by her private client Madame Ogata to murder husbands committing domestic violence. After they rescue a tortured teenage girl who escapes from the cult Sakigake ('Forerunner'), a plan to assassinate the Leader is fixed. Tengo, alternatively, is a mathematics teacher at a cram school and a part-time column writer. He is recruited by editor Komatsu to rewrite the draft novella *Air Chrysalis* (*Kūki sanagi*) about life in Sakigake by Fuka-Eri, a teenage girl who also escaped from the cult, making it a prize-winner and bestseller. When Tengo is pursued by the cult for the novella and Aomame too for the assassination, they, reunited, finally escape from 1Q84 and return to 1984.

The Little People are creatures in the novella *Air Chrysalis*. The heroine is locked up for ten days with the corpse of a goat she fails to care for. At night, the Little People come out of the goat's mouth and start to make an Air Chrysalis. The confinement ends before the Chrysalis is finished, hence the girl never knows what may come out. At first Tengo thinks it is all the result of Fuka-Eri's imagination, but she insists the Little People *actually* existed. She suggests that the Little People are godlike for Sakigake, who receive information from them. They are omnipresent and omniscient:

> 'They are watching us,' Fuka-Eri said.
> 'You mean the Little People?' Tengo asked.
> Fuka-Eri did not answer him.
> 'They know we're here,' Tengo said.
> 'Of course they know,' Fuka-Eri said.
> 'What are they trying to do to us?'
> 'They can't do anything to us.'
> 'That's good.'
> 'For now, that is' (ibid: 459).

The Little People observe Tengo and Fuka-Eri, cause thunderstorms to express their anger, but they do no direct harm to people. Their mere existence is enough to deter, as those aware of their power automatically reflect over their actions repeatedly, wondering if they are 'correct' (*seikaku*) and fearing any possible annoyance and consequential revenge to their beloved. The Little People in this sense work like surveillance cameras, who are only concerned about people around Sakigake because they control and manipulate the cult to fulfil their will. Professor Ebisuno, the protector of Fuka-Eri, hits the essence of the influence of the Little People:

> George Orwell introduced the dictator Big Brother in his novel *1984*, as I'm sure you know. The book was an allegorical treatment of Stalinism, of course. And ever since then, the term 'Big Brother' has functioned as a social icon. That was Orwell's great accomplishment. But now, in the real year 1984, Big

PAPER

Brother is all too famous, and all too obvious. If Big Brother were to appear before us now, we'd point to him and say, 'Watch out! He's Big Brother!' There's no longer any place for a Big Brother in this real world of ours. Instead, these so-called Little People have come on the scene. Interesting verbal contrast, don't you think? (ibid: 236).

'Little People' are 'Big Brother' in *1Q84*, only in a physically smaller and structurally more fragmentary way. Like Orwell, Murakami reminds readers to rethink the meaning and effects of surveillance, as well as how it may change our sense of reality. That they became a part of everyday life for people in Sakigake, Fuka-Eri and Tengo marks the difference between *1Q84* and *Nineteen Eighty-Four*; 'Better be careful in the forest,' Fuka-Eri reminds Tengo (Murakami 2011: 300).

Compared with *Nineteen Eighty-Four*, *1Q84* becomes an alienated duplication of the original world, as if a model of David Lyon's 'surveillance society' (1994, 2001), Chalmers' society 'acculturated to, and saturated with, surveillance' (2005: 262), or Dilevko's 'new surveilled world whose aim is to channel behaviour into normalised and thus easily manageable patterns' (2011: 117). *Nineteen Eighty-Four* and *1Q84* for Aomame and Tengo are Murakami's 'Reality A' and 'Reality B' (2010), or 'this world' (*kotchi no sekai*) and 'that world' (*atchi no sekai*) (Amitrano 2015: 207). 'This world', *our* world, is factual, while 'that world' is fictional. It is the objectification under surveillance and control of the Little People that reduces 'the level of reality' (in Murakami's words, 2010) of *1Q84* and makes it 'that world'. In 'that world' manipulated by the Little People, people are simplified into labels, instrumentalised and used. Just as those in *Nineteen Eighty-Four*, they lose control of their fate. 'I'm just following the plan that has already been laid out. Continuing to live, alone, in this unreasonable world ... where something called Little People control the destiny of others,' thought Aomame to herself (Murakami 2011: 610). Everything in *1Q84* has been – and must be – controlled and designed by the Little People. That was why Aomame and Tengo do not belong to 'that world', and why even their returning to 'this world' is also a part of their destiny. 'To make sure the Little People don't harm you, you have to find something the Little People don't have,' Fuka-Eri tells Tengo (ibid: 300).

SURVEILLANCE AS AN EXPERIENCE AND SURVEILLANCE AS A PREMISE

Dystopia has been a common theme for indie game developers. Games take a different approach from novels to narrate and present. Juul's discussion about the 'chronologicity' of games (2001), Dovey's argument that games are 'activities' (2006: 23), and Newman's opinion that games are 'audiovisual spectacles'

(2008: 46) suggest that 'ludonarrative' strategies and multimedia involvement enable games to be a more direct, immersive and modern medium to represent modern surveillance 'beyond Orwell' (Lyon 2007: 143). The four games to be discussed are all inspired by the Orwellian dystopia, especially *Orwell: Keeping an Eye on You* (Osmotic 2016), which names its episodes after famous quotes from the novel. According to Tadhg Kelly's categories (2011), the four games can be classified into two types of gameplay: one behaviourist, focusing more on the action of surveillance itself and employing the player as a literal observer, document-checker and governmental officer; the other 'narrativist', concentrating more on storytelling and involving the player as an important participant with potential to make changes happen. Though different in gameplay style, all games portray the player as both the subject and the object, both the executor and the victim of surveillance. The means and focus of surveillance are updated from *Nineteen Eighty-Four*, but the purpose and harm remain the same.

Papers, Please (Pope 2013) and *Beholder* (Warm Lamp 2016) belong to the first category. To be clear, in *Papers* the player becomes the O'Brien of *Nineteen Eighty-Four*, while in *Beholder*, they are Mr. Charrington, the landlord of Smith and Juliet's love nest. In both games, the player works as a governmental worker, checking the paperwork of travellers and immigrants at the border checkpoint or in disguise as a benign landlord supervising the behaviour of tenants, ready to report or blackmail them at any time. In addition, the player has to shoulder the responsibility for taking care of their family, paying house rent or tuition fee for their child. The familial responsibility requires them to consider the balance between selflessness and selfishness with great caution. If they allow people lacking proper immigrant documents to enter the country to reunite with family, they will be fined for the dereliction of duty. If they do not frame or blackmail an innocent tenant to raise money for their daughter's illness, she will die in their arms.

What *Papers* and *Beholder* inherit from *Nineteen Eighty-Four*, apart from the representation of a surveillance society, is the criticism of the objectification of people and the subsequent warning of the banality of evil. *Papers* completely objectifies the player as an inspecting machine. To earn their family food and heat, they must repeat daily the mechanical work of accessing personal information and comparing paperwork with the latest immigrant policies. Both the officer whom the player plays and the people being checked are objectified in this process. The player becomes both the accomplice to totalitarianism, who assists and reinforces its reign simply by following the rules and undertaking their duty, and the victim to it, since they are also objectified, and their loyalty to their job is justifiable. The dilemma in *Beholder* is even more dramatic. As the developers of *Beholder* point out: 'You are just a cog in a totalitarian machine – a cog that has been given the power to destroy the privacy of any person' (Alawar 2019). 'The Ministry can turn a blind eye to forgery and blackmail if they help you achieve your goal,' the player is thus instructed in *Beholder* when introduced to their duty. When surveillance cameras endow the player omniscience, that the authorities 'turn a blind eye to forgery and blackmail' endows the player with omnipotence. This is exactly what worries Richards about surveillance society: it enhances 'the watcher's ability to blackmail, coerce and discriminate against the people under its scrutiny' (2013: 1936).

As the power of vision transfers into a power of action, surveillance not only represents totalitarianism, but also works in effect as totalitarianism itself; once the executor of surveillance becomes the 'cog in a totalitarian machine' using and abusing the power of the system – not necessarily out of a sinister purpose – they will fall into the trap of 'the banality of evil' (Arendt 2006 [1963]). Arendt's discussion focuses more on the lack of 'thinking' in the process of totalitarianism as seen in *Papers*, but *Beholder* thinking is completely invalidated. One *cannot* think, so evil, instead of a choice, becomes the foundation of this totalitarian world. The 'choices' the player make are not out of free will but forced by the system: not reporting those suspected by the government but who are actually innocent, the player will be arrested and eliminated for shielding a suspect. To protect their children from school dropout or fatal illness, the player must blackmail the tenants for an extra income. Each test of power and human nature further blurs the boundary between good and evil, which ends up disappearing. The 'right' choices are always 'wrong', and vice versa. The player will forget about morality, following only the rules and their interests. The character stripped of 'perspicacity, of psychological instinct' is thus objectified into an evil 'automaton' and 'symbol' (Cioran 2015: 85).

Replica (Somi 2016) and *Orwell* give the player more initiative: they experience surveillance rather than exercise surveillance, and for the player, surveillance is neither carried simply *by* them nor *on* them, but *through* them. In both games, the player is outside the totalitarian system, an employed and authorised inspector working in modern society detecting mobile phones, SNS, and anti-government activists. *Replica* is fully based on a mobile phone, while *Orwell* employs a system called 'Orwell', which gathers all public information left on the internet and hacks into devices, reading text messages and eavesdropping on phone calls. Compared with all other works mentioned above, both games introduce more advanced technology to execute a very modern system of surveillance. It not only watches, but also collects all abstract information about a person from favourite food to sexuality.

But even the player, the 'outsider', is *inside* the system: the observer is also observed. Surveillance in *Replica* is, from the beginning, Foucauldian and works via self-surveillance. 'Always remember that we are watching you and your family,' the player is told (Somi 2016). Any violation of command can lead to a threatening call and end up with the player in jail. This is 'a system of ubiquitous spying … everybody may be a police agent and each individual feels himself under constant surveillance' (Arendt 2017 [1951]). The player observes the characters; the government observes the player; the player also observes and acts to avoid being arrested. In *Orwell*, however, the transformation of the nature of surveillance from Benthamian to Foucauldian is the key point. After the characters realise they are being observed by the player, they will instruct the player to find an entry in the system recording all actions of the players. As Wasihun points out, admitting that the watcher is also watched 'entails a renegotiation of power' (2016: 387). When the player reveals to the nation that it is under close governmental surveillance, people protest and demonstrate. 'Orwell' is finally cancelled.

Once the player has been appointed as the executor of surveillance in a totalitarian society, it is hard for a game to avoid dragging the player into the trap of 'the banality of evil', as *Papers* and *Beholder* do. Yet *Replica* and *Orwell* cleverly create a space outside – beyond – the game. Though the embodiment of the player in the virtual game has no room to think about good and evil, the players *themselves* are able to think in the *authentic* world. Both games have 'metagame' elements,[5] as the virtual characters realise the existence of the inspector/the player and directly resort to them for help. On the one hand, the information that the player has already gathered about the characters is plausible enough for them to sympathise and imagine the characters as authentic persons; yet on the other hand, the help-seeking directly drags the player into the world of the game and makes them one of the characters as well. From either perspective, the player jumps from Reality A into Reality B just as Aomame entered *1Q84* from 1984. 'To make sure the Little People don't harm you, you have to find something the Little People don't have' (Murakami 2011: 300). A *character* in the world of Reality B, as in *Papers* or *Beholder*, may easily sink into the banality of evil, lacking the ability or power to think, yet a *player* from Reality A can think. As the game simulates real life (McMahan 2007: 167), it temporarily limits the player's thinking, but after all it is a pseudo-reality 'other than life' (Atkins 2003: 142). When reminded of their authentic reality where no surveillance exists, the player's power to think, evaluate and choose is immediately restored. That is what characters from the virtual world 'don't have'.

Replica and *Orwell* seem to offer a realistic suggestion for the watched to resist against the surveillance – to resort to an outside, benign force – but in reality it is simply not workable. Though I have listed possible good endings of the two games, in which the characters are saved and the totalitarian governments are either overturned or restructured, the possibility of bad endings is held in the hands of the player as well. They can also choose to report the characters, in which case they will be investigated, convicted and arrested, while the player will obtain a game achievement. This, for sure, does not suggest that the developers encourage the player to support totalitarianism and be an active reporter. What they present is the process and possibilities of surveillance, not a straightforward answer to the boundary between good and evil or the definition of morality. We may recall the short interruption of surveillance during the replacement of one totalitarian regime with another in *1985*. On one hand, surveillance exists as long as totalitarianism exists; on the other, surveillance exists as long as its subjects and objects obey. 'You MUST! But WILL YOU???' (Alawar 2018) asked the makers of *Beholder* to the player. The same question may also be asked to the characters in and readers/players of *Nineteen Eighty-Four*, *1985*, and *Papers*, who struggle with the moral dilemmas, unable to decide on the boundaries between good and evil. But the author of *1Q84* and the makers of *Replica*, and *Orwell* certainly ask a different question: 'You CAN! But MUST YOU???' What they attempt to imagine is not only the form and harm of surveillance, but also how one can jump out from the dilemma and break away from surveillance.

CONCLUSION

Inspired by George Orwell's *Nineteen Eighty-Four*, popular culture increasingly and extensively investigates the techniques and possibility of surveillance, as well as its embodiment. Surveillance in *Nineteen Eighty-Four* is a mixed model of the Benthamian and Foucauldian panopticon that objectifies its people and drags them into the mire of banal evil. Novels and games inspired by *1984* extend or transfer the idea of surveillance for their own purposes: *1985* by Dalos György explores the phases of surveillance and its relationship with totalitarianism concerning his personal history, while *1Q84* by Murakami Haruki imagines an alternative reality influenced by surveillance and, like Orwell, encourages the readers to reconsider surveillance. Games, on the other hand, take advantage of multimedia and simulation to extend the implication of surveillance into a more inclusive and modern sense. *Papers, Please* and *Beholder* portray an all-round totalitarian society under surveillance and warn about the trap of the banality of evil, while *Replica* and *Orwell* attempt to seek a possible exit from it by encouraging individual thought. So increasingly the notions of 'surveillance' and 'Orwellian society' are used as a shortcut to criticise, warn, remind – or simply describe.

NOTES

[1] For *1984*'s reference to history and concerns about reality, see Orwell's letter to Henson on 16 June 1949, in worries about 'totalitarian ideas' (Orwell and Angus 1968: 502). Also see e.g. Booker 1994: 69-90; Kateb 1971; Lewis 1981: 102-116; Sandison 1986 for a general background of *Nineteen Eighty-Four*; Freedman 1984; Newsinger 2018; Hunt 2013 for Orwell's political ideas in the novel; Stansky and Abrahams 1994, Woodcock 1970: 47-175 for his personal life and *Nineteen Eighty-Four*

[2] Scholarship on Dalos, though little, reads the novel as a literalisation and a sarcastic criticism of his life and the history of Hungary during the '60s and '70s. See Booker 1994: 114-116 and Gottlieb 2001: 260-261

[3] For the theme of *1Q84*, see e.g. Franssen 2018; Ilis 2017; Kawade 2009; Ozaki 2009; Strecher 2011

[4] Scholarship on the connection between *Nineteen Eighty-Four* and *1Q84* largely mentions only superficial phenomena, namely the connection of the novel's name (as in Japanese '9' and 'Q' share the identical pronunciation) and the connection of a key character's name ('Big Brother' in *Nineteen Eighty-Four* and 'Little People' in *1Q84*). See, for example, Amitrano 2015: 212-213; Ilis 2017; Yeung 2017. Discussion on other aspects is rarely seen

[5] Metagame, not to be confused with Nigel Howard's mathematical metagame theory, is a game type inspired by metafiction. In general, it tends to create an awareness of game-playing instead of an immersive or simulative experience. A metagame has quasi-self-awareness, declares to players that it is a game, and/or asks players to decide upon information not only given in the game but also beyond the game in their actual life. Famous metagames include *The Stanley Parable* (Davey Wreden 2011), *The Magic Circle* (Question 2015), *Undertale* (Toby Fox 2015) and *Doki Doki Literature Club!* (Team Salvato 2017). Some card games e.g. *Yu-Gi-Oh!* (Konami 1999-present) are also a type of megagame. See, for example, Boluk and Lemieux 2017 for metagame theories; Garfield 2010; Jie 2016; and Yoge 2017 for metagame criticism

REFERENCES

PRIMARY SOURCES AND LUDOLOGY

Dalos, György (1983 [1981]) *1985: A Historical Report (Hongkong 2036) from the Hungarian of **** (trans. by Hood, Stuart and Schmid, Estella), London: Pluto

Dalos, György (2011) *1985* (trans. by Yu, Zemin), Shanghai: Shanghai Renmin Press

Murakami, Haruki (2011) *1Q84* (trans. by Rubin, Jay and Gabriel, Philip), London: Harvill Secker

Orwell, George (1954 [1949]) *Nineteen Eighty-Four*, Harmondsworth: Penguin

Osmotic Studios (2016) *Orwell: Keeping an Eye on You*

Pope, Lucas (2013) *Papers, Please*

Somi (2016) *Replica*

Warm Lamp Games (2016) *Beholder*

SECONDARY SOURCES AND CRITICISM

Alawar Premium (2018) BEHOLDER press kit. Available online at https://beholder-game.com/en/presskit, accessed on 10 May 2019

Alawar Premium (2019) BEHOLDER: Every choice has consequences. Available online at https://beholder-game.com, accessed on 10 May 2019

Amitrano, Giorgia and Amitrano, Giorgio (2015). Books within books: Literary references in Murakami Haruki's fiction, *Japanese Language and Literature*, No. 49, No. 1 pp 201-220

Arendt, Hannah (2006 [1963]) *Eichmann in Jerusalem*, New York: Penguin. Available online from the National Library of Scotland

Arendt, Hannah (2017 [1951]) *The Origins of Totalitarianism*, New York: Penguin. Available online from the National Library of Scotland

Atkins, Barry (2003) *More than a Game: The Computer Game as Fictional Form*, Manchester: Manchester University Press

Bentham, Jeremy (1843 [1791]) *Panopticon: Or, The Inspection-House*, Bowring, John (ed.) *The Works of Jeremy Bentham, Vol. 4*, Edinburgh: William Tait. Available online at https://books.google.co.uk/books?id=QdEQAAAAYAAJ, accessed on 10 May 2019

Bloom, Harold (1987) Introduction, Bloom, Harold (ed.) *George Orwell's 1984*, Langhorne, PA: Chelsea House pp 1-7

Boluk, Stephanie and Lemieux, Patrick (2017) *Metagaming: Playing, Competing, Spectating, Cheating, Trading, Making and Breaking Videogames*, Minneapolis, MN: University of Minnesota Press

Booker, M. Keith (1994) *The Dystopian Impulse in Modern Literature: Fiction as Social Criticism*, Westport, CT: Greenwood

CBS (2011) *Person of interest*

Chalmers, Robert (2005) Orwell or all well? The rise of surveillance culture, *Alternative Law Journal*, Vol. 30, No. 6 pp 258-262

Cioran, E. M. (2015) *History and Utopia*, (trans. by Howard, Richard) US: Arcade

Dilevko, Juris (2011) Destroying individuality and freedom in the name of technophilia, *Journal of Information Ethics*, Vol. 20, No. 1 pp 113-120

Dovey, Jon and Kennedy, Helen W. (2006) *Game Cultures: Computer Games as New Media*, Berkshire: Open University Press

Elmer, Greg (2012) Panopticon – discipline – control, Ball, Kirstie et al. (eds) *Routledge Handbook of Surveillance Studies*, London: Routledge pp 21-29

Foucault, Michel (1991 [1975]) *Discipline and Punish: The Birth of the Prison* (trans. by Sheridan, Alan), London: Penguin

Franssen, Gaston (2018) The literary auto-representation of Haruki Murakami: Rewriting celebrity authorship in *1Q84*, *Celebrity Studies*, Vol. 9, No. 2 pp 264-270

Freedman, Carl (1984) Antinomies of *Nineteen Eighty-Four*, *Modern Fiction Studies*, Vol. 30, No. 4 pp 601-620

Garfield, Richard (2010) Lost in the shuffle: Games within games, *MTG*, 21 June. Available online at https://magic.wizards.com/en/articles/archive/feature/lost-shuffle-games-within-games-2010-06-21-0, accessed on 10 May 2019

Gottlieb, Erika (2001) *Dystopian Fiction East and West: Universe of Terror and Trial*, Quebec: McGill-Queen's University Press

Hunt, William (2013) Orwell's *Commedia*: The ironic theology of *Nineteen Eighty-Four*, *Modern Philology*, Vol. 110, No. 4 pp 536-563

Kawade Shobō Shinsha, Publishers (2009) *Murakami Haruki 1Q84 wo dōu yomu ka* [*How to Read Murakami Haruki's* 1Q84] (trans. by Hou, Wei and Wei, Dahai), Jinan: Shandong Literature and Art Publishing House

Ilis, Florina (2017) Towards a post-human condition of the bQdy in Haruki Murakami's *1Q84*: From grief to nostalgia (trans. by Chiorean, Anca), *Philobiblon*, No. 22, Vol. 2 pp 175-186

Jiewaimoalikesi (2016) Gushi beihoude gushi: Dang 'Meta' yujian 'youxi' [Story behind the story: When 'Meta' meets 'game'], *Indienova*, 5 April. Available online at https://indienova.com/indie-game-development/meta-meet-game/, accessed on 10 May 2019.

Juul, Jesper (2001) Games telling stories? – A brief note on games and narratives, *Game Studies*, Vol. 1, No. 1. Available online at http://gamestudies.org/0101/juul-gts/, accessed on 10 May 2019.

Kateb, George (1971) The road to *1984*, Hynes, Samuel (eds) *Twentieth Century Interpretations of 1984*, Englewood Cliffs, NJ: Prentice-Hall pp 73-87

Kelly, Tadhg (2011) *The Four Lenses of Game Making*. Available online at https://www.whatgamesare.com/2011/12/the-four-lenses-of-game-making.html, accessed on 10 May 2019

Lewis, Peter (1981) *George Orwell: The Road to 1984*, London: Heinemann Quixote

Lianos, Michalis (2010) Periopticon: Control beyond freedom and coercion – And two possible advancements in the social sciences, Haggerty, Kevin D. and Samatas, Minas (eds) *Surveillance and Democracy*, NY: Routledge pp 69-88

Lyon, David (1994) *The Electronic Eye: The Rise of Surveillance Society*, Cambridge: Polity

Lyon, David (2001) *Surveillance Society: Monitoring Everyday Life*, Berkshire: Open University Press

Lyon, David (2007) *Surveillance Studies: An Overview*, Cambridge: Polity

Marx, Gary T. (2007) What's new about the 'new surveillance'? Classifying for change and continuity, Hier, Sean P. and Greenberg, Josh (eds) *The Surveillance Studies Reader*, Berkshire: Open University Press pp 82-94

McMahan, Alison (2007) *Second Life*: The game of virtual life, Atkins, Barry and Krzywinska, Tanya (eds) *Vidoegame, Player, Text*, Manchester: Manchester University Press pp 158-174

Murakami, Haruki. (2010) Reality A. and Reality B. (trans. by Rubin, Jay) *New York Times*, 29 November. Available online at http://www.nytimes.com/2010/12/02/opinion/global/02iht-GA06-Murakami.html, accessed on 10 May 2019

Newman, James (2008) *Playing with Videogames*. London: Routledge

Newsinger, John (2018) *Hope Lies in the Proles: George Orwell and the Left*, London: Pluto

Ōi, kōichi (2009) Murakami Haruki shi *1Q84* wo kataru, raika wo medo ni dai 3 bu [Murakami Haruki on *1Q84*, Volume 3 forthcoming], *Mainichi Shimbun*, 17 September. Available online at https://www.douban.com/group/topic/8033417/, accessed on 10 May 2019

Orwell, Sonia, and Angus, Ian (1968) *The Collected Essays, Journalism and Letters of George Orwell, Vol. IV, In Front of Your Nose: 1945-1950*, London: Secker and Warburg

Osmotic Studios (2016) *Orwell: Keeping an Eye on You*, out now for PC and Mac. Available online at http://www.osmoticstudios.com/orwell-keeping-an-eye-on-you, accessed on 10 May 2019.

Ozaki, Mariko (2009) *1Q84* e no sanjūnen: Murakami Haruki shi intabyū [Thirty years towards *1Q84*: Interviewing Mr Murakami Haruki] (trans. by Mucaocao et al.), *Yomiuri Shimbun*, 16-18 June. Available online at https://site.douban.com/167438/widget/notes/9122416/note/310057628/, accessed on 10 May 2019

Richards, Neil M. (2013) The dangers of surveillance, *Harvard Law Review*, Vol. 126, No. 7 pp 1934-1965

Sandison, Alan (1986) *George Orwell: After 1984*, Hampshire: MacMillan, second edition.

Spender, Stephen (1971) Introduction to *1984*, Hynes, Samuel (eds) *Twentieth Century Interpretations of* 1984, Englewood Cliffs, NJ: Prentice-Hall pp 62-72

Stansky, Peter and Abrahams, William (1994) *The Unknown Orwell*, London: Constable

Strecher, Matthew (2011). At the critical stage: A report on the state of Murakami Haruki studies, *Literature Compass*, Vol. 8, No. 11 pp 856-869

Wasihun, Betiel (2016) Surveillance narratives: Kafka, Orwell, and Ulrich Peltzer's Post-9/11 novel *Teil der Lösung*, *A Journal of Germanic Studies*, Vol. 52, No. 4 pp 382-406

Williams, Ian (2017) *Political and Cultural Perceptions of George Orwell*, New York: Palgrave Macmillan

Woodcock, George (1970) *The Crystal Spirit: A Study of George Orwell*, Harmondsworth: Penguin

Yeo, Michael (2010) Propaganda and surveillance in George Orwell's *Nineteen Eighty-Four*: Two sides of the same coin, *Global Media Journal*, Vol. 3, No. 2 pp 49-66

Yeung, Virginia (2017) Stories within stories: A study of narrative embedding in Haruki Murakami's *1Q84*, *Critique: Studies in Contemporary Fiction*, Vol. 58, No. 4 pp 426-436

Yoge (2017) Metagame: Chaoyue youxi de youxi: Nainiu jingxuan Vol. 16 [Metagame: The game beyond game: Cow's Selection Vol. 16], *CowLevel*, 16 June. Available online at https://cowlevel.net/article/1869436, accessed on 10 May 2019

NOTE ON THE CONTRIBUTOR

Xiaozhou Li is a postgraduate student in Museum Studies at UCL. She has acquired her BA in English from Tsinghua University and MScRes from the University of Edinburgh. Her academic interests include British Romanticism, literature and game and material culture.

PAPER

The Unconscious on Screen:
Psychoanalytic Themes in Michael Radford's adaptation of *Nineteen Eighty-Four*

JAMES JARRETT

This paper aims to present a structuralist and psychoanalytic analysis of how the director Michael Radford exploits the medium of film to convey the richness of Orwell's vision of the future in Nineteen Eighty-Four. *The thematic importance of betrayal is conveyed through Winston Smith's troubled relations with his external world of social interaction and his internal world of illusion and phantasy. The paper ends by arguing that Radford demonstrates, perhaps unwittingly, how and why INGSOC's attempt to crush humanity by controlling hearts and minds must fail in the end. Winston has been successfully brainwashed by the Party. But history shows that systems based on illogical nonsense, fear and repression do not last indefinitely. The spirit of conscious and unconscious human love, and our need to search for freedom, reason, logic and truth will endure, even in the face of our most fearful nightmares.*

Keywords: Orwell, *1984*, Radford, psychoanalysis, film

Let the purists baulk! Our beliefs about celebrated authors are not pure, but received, refracted through the many lenses of popular culture. Moreover, the artistic contributions of others, working across the creative spectrum, often enhance, rather than denude, a literary work of its value. Essentially, there is nothing inherently vulgar about a film adaptation of a great novel, and it is not necessarily the case that a cinematic interpretation of a work can only ever be a pale imitation of the 'real thing' – the cherished and sacrosanct written word. The act of reading alone, in splendid isolation, may be a pleasurable form of intellectual enrichment, but is it not also a little solipsistic? Is it not predicated on the problematic assumption that the dyadic relationship between reader and text is inviolable and that nothing else could, or should, intervene? My answer to these questions is to assert that the dramatic arts, in both the theatre and on screen, can illuminate the shadowy corners of a 'great' text and enhance its reputation. A visionary film director or designer can draw out the colours of a novel: providing a vivid level of visual detail, complexity and specificity. George Orwell's lucid works of political, social and prophetic historical insight have been

JAMES
JARRETT

adapted for stage and screen on several occasions. In this paper I aim to present a structuralist and psychoanalytic analysis of how the director Michael Radford exploits the medium of film to convey the richness of Orwell's vision of the future in *Nineteen Eighty-Four*.

Adapting *Nineteen Eighty-Four* for the big screen presents a series of creative, intellectual and ethical challenges. Orwell helps us by providing a detailed description of London, the capital of 'Airstrip 1', and Michael Radford's version faithfully brings the decay, destruction and squalor of Winston Smith's world to a movie audience with a commendable level of realism, grit and detail. But one is still left with a problem: how can we translate so many words into a powerful visual narrative without doing a disservice to Orwell's writing?

Radford achieves success by choosing to focus on Winston's own need to piece together his past and to bring to consciousness his own unconscious phantasies and neuroses. Moreover, as Winston writes in his diary, his thoughts and feelings collide with his memories and fantasies to engender a pattern of free association,[1] not dissimilar to that of a psychoanalytic therapy session. In this sense, the film explores Winston's growing belief that O'Brien will, somehow, assist him in this process, and ends with his tragic betrayal at the hands of the inner party honcho (in one dream-like sequence Winston even imagines O'Brien to be calling out to him with an invitation to 'Meet in a place where there is no darkness').

Thus, in *Nineteen Eighty-Four*, the state's relentless surveillance of Winston's daily activities has not supressed his need to interrogate his own mind, to uncover the truth about his own past and to construct his own identity. Indeed, whilst in the novel Orwell thoroughly explicates the nature of Winston's circumstances, Radford's film employs a blend of image, sound and camera movement to develop its thematic points of emphasis. In effect, Winston's own intelligent, intuitive, whispering voice emerges clearly through a cacophony of utterances that relentlessly command, inspire and confess.

THE POWER OF NIGHTMARES: 'SHOUT, SHOUT, SHOUT OUT HIS NAME!'

Clearly influenced by documentary footage of Nazi and fascist rallies, Radford's depiction of an INGSOC assembly in the opening scene is an astute illustration of Orwell's vision. The Party film begins with a romantic image of an INGSOC flag fluttering in a light breeze, complete with its central logo of two hands shaking – one black and one white – mythologising the nation as a land of equality, fraternity and peace. Indeed, Radford's application of an uplifting musical score, when combined with a stirring montage of cinematic images depicting 'Oceania' as a glorious utopia of energetic plenty, creates a tragic and absurd counterpoint to the reality of the people's brutal political and intellectual oppression as well as their abject economic and cultural poverty. The propaganda footage, which suggests an athletic and dynamic nation, in the pink of youthful, vigorous health, contrasts with Radford's image of rows and rows of pathetic, flabby, destitute slaves whose sedentary minds and bodies are crumbling like the buildings they inhabit. The visual grammar of moving images is supported by an overlay of didactic speech, uttered by a faceless narrator who softly patronises the ignorant assembly with a pompous summary of the land and its people:

> This is our land. A land of peace and of plenty. A land of harmony and hope. This is our land. Oceania. These are our people. The workers. The strivers. The builders. These are our people. That built our world (Radford *1984*).

Through the strategic assemblage of film images, INGSOC cunningly exploits Old Testament mythology to inspire and indoctrinate the people, depicting Oceania as a majestic wilderness – a Garden of Eden brilliantly tamed by the technological ingenuity of man. But this land is clearly not a 'heaven on earth' built by the back-breaking, bare-handed toil of a race of noble and industrious heroes. On the contrary, it is a regressive, pathological prison of the mind, body and soul, where all notions or conceptualisations of individualism, or individuality, have been crushed.

The seamless transition from mythicised images of a serene, productive society, to the gratuitously realistic depiction of the terrifying carnage of the modern battle field, lend to the entire experience the peculiar sensation of a dream – or perhaps more pertinently – *a nightmare*. The aggressively anti-semitic introduction on the big screen of a recorded image of the scapegoated 'Goldstein' (is he, or was he, ever a *real* person?) violently shifts the tone and atmosphere of the event, stimulating the audience into screaming insults and vilification at a despised face whose words they cannot hear and who – absurdly - cannot hear them. The narrator tells the audience that:

> Even we grasp at victory, there is a cancer, an evil tumour, growing, *spreading*, in our midst. Shout! *Shout!* Shout out his name! (Radford *1984*).

The intensity of this bizarre and disturbing frenzy of hatred is captured as Radford focuses on the visceral faces of the baying mob. The participants also exhibit a superstitious fantasy that their enemies can be nullified by thrusting their arms into the air to make a 'cross', in a 'magic'[2] gesture redolent of Christian ritualism and iconography.

JAMES JARRETT

In essence, the final image is of a whole society reduced to the horrifying inequity of wretched servitude through fear and ignorance; a failed and miserable dystopia where human beings are cultivated like animals or vegetables. Indeed, the hall itself, bathed in darkness and teeming with bodies, is uncannily reminiscent of an industrial produce farm where humans are treated like fungi, 'kept in the dark and fed on manure'.[3] Radford symbolises the brutal destruction of the individual by clothing the outer party members in blue overalls. The degradingly austere utilitarianism and industrialism of this uniform perhaps comments ironically on the failed technocratic dream of the party's founding members – whilst exemplifying the crude methods they employ to deny the individual a personal identity.

Although it is clear that we are watching an extremely well-rehearsed and practised ritual, still its theatrical elements of active and demonstrable audience participation are adhered to by an energetic and enthusiastic crowd. In fact, one particular young woman is so eager to impress: in a moment of over-exuberance she hurls what appears to be a book at the image of Goldstein, thereby attracting an insouciant glance from inner party enforcer O'Brien. Simultaneously, Winston, who is seated amongst the audience and who seems to have been watching the entire spectacle unfold in slightly confused silence, also notices Julia's outburst as well as O'Brien's casual glance. This incident, which appears to pass unnoticed by the crowd as their verbal 'attack' on Goldstein reaches a crescendo, nevertheless establishes the narrative connection between Winston, Julia and O'Brien. Moreover, it subtly presages the dramatic tension of the film, anticipating the coming conflict between its three central characters.

THE WORLD OF WINSTON SMITH

Soon, we see Winston hurriedly returning to his flat after work, picking his way through the grey, bombed-out streets of London. The mountains of masonry, debris and rubble are suggestive of a recent air raid and again speak to the absurdity of the Party depiction of Oceania as a 'land of peace' in their propaganda film.

Once inside his cell-like apartment, Winston's every move is tracked and evaluated by the omniscient telescreen. He reaches to light a cigarette and suddenly realises that the tobacco has slipped from the flimsy paper. His annoyed and frustrated reaction – to mutter 'bugger' under his breath – is a miniscule flicker of insurrection, so small that the auditory mechanism of the telescreen cannot detect it. However, it is nonetheless significant since it signifies, beyond the suffocation of his life as an INGSOC slave, that Winston is preoccupied with his own bodily comfort and needs.

Again, Radford draws our attention to the blatant ridiculousness in the contrast between INGSOC'S fantasy vision of Oceania as plentiful and abundant and the crushing destitution and indignity of Winston's material circumstances. The tragic and comic absurdity of an intelligent but sickly man with a hacking cough, scraping around in an attempt to meet his most basic needs, in a world where everything is broken, damaged or scarce, brings to mind the tragic comic plays of Samuel Beckett;[4] much less the party's Nietzschean propaganda of the Oceanic 'Superman',[5] striding forth through the nation's resplendent fields of golden, swaying corn.

Having been born into war, destitution, sickness and slavery, it is not surprising that Winston hopes that one day, somehow, he may be able to live a better life in a better world. This forlorn aspiration is symbolised in the latent wish of a recurring dream. Before Winston, Radford depicts a glorious countryside vista of rolling hills – a colourful and majestic scene redolent of a beautiful summer's day in rural England. Winston *seems* to turn this dream into a reality later when he meets Julia in secret (although it is unclear how much of this experience is real or imagined).

Because INGSOC cannot detect silent 'thoughtcrime' in sleep, the liberating effects of this dream perhaps motivate Winston in his desperate fight to salvage whatever humanity, sanity and hope for the future he may have left. Indeed: to be able to contemplate the possibility that such a wondrous place might exist without ruthlessly admonishing oneself for committing the heinous act of 'thoughtcrime' is a joyful and ecstatic meditation. It is also an antidote to the gratingly naive imbecility of the deluded Parsons and the obsessive, yet regressive, intellectual tyranny of Syme, who revels in the horror of Newspeak's obliteration of words.

BETRAYAL: 'UNDERNEATH THE SPREADING CHESTNUT TREE…'

Ever since the extensive dissemination of the New Testament throughout Europe, the notion of 'betrayal' has played an important conceptual role in the development of a moral and ethical framework for Western social and cultural relations. Psychoanalysis rejects the Christian account of betrayal and, instead, focuses on the child's relations with its earliest loved 'object', the mother. The first sensation of having been 'betrayed' emerges in relation to the oedipal crisis where the infant feels forsaken having conceptualised the presence of the father inside the object of the mother. If these feelings cannot be adequately resolved, the deleterious effects of unconscious pain persist.

Throughout Radford's film, the thematic importance of betrayal is conveyed through Winston's troubled relations with his external world of social interaction and his internal world of illusion and phantasy. When Winston writes in his diary, he knows that to do so

JAMES JARRETT

means death, not the *threat* of death if discovered. For, although there is a rebellious human instinct within Winston to stay alive and survive the horrors of INGSOC, he is also clear in his own mind that this is nothing but a delusion. Defying the Party can only lead to torture and, ultimately, annihilation. Thus, like a wretched character from a tragedy by Sophocles,[6] Winston knows that he will not be able to exculpate himself and elude his fate. Therefore, the lucid image in his dreams of walking down a dark corridor towards a door that leads to 'Room 101' is a grim premonition that predicts his demise.

Furthermore, an uneasy sense of foreboding and portentousness is illustrated in Winston's remembrance of a popular piece of music from the 1930s. We hear him reprise these words on several occasions throughout the film. Glenn Miller's version of an old English ditty 'The Chestnut Tree', is a jaunty and playful song that evokes the joy of adolescent love:

> But, underneath the spreading chestnut tree
>
> I loved her and she loved me
>
> There she used to sit upon my knee
>
> Neath the spreading chestnut tree (https://lyricsplayground.com/alpha/songs).

But when Winston recites the song's lyrics, he changes the second line to 'I sold you, and you sold me' (Radford *1984*). Of course, the Chestnut Tree itself is a café situated near Winston's digs in London. And yet, initially, like an elliptical or abstruse message entwined within the imagery of a dream, the full meaning of Winston's rhyme is unclear. However, it later becomes apparent that it expresses, amongst other things, Winston's painful acceptance that – no matter how much he might try to resist the impulse – when captured he will betray Julia. He will 'sell her down the river'[7] by begging his tormentor to inflict the worst possible fate imaginable *on her* – and she will do the same *to him*.

Equally, being *underneath the spreading chestnut tree* brings to mind Winston and Julia's love making, their 'primal scene'[8] that plays out in the seclusion of the woods. Radford's depiction of this daringly passionate and exhausting encounter is uncompromising, as well as being challenging for audiences of the time. The film's slow motion images of Julia, wantonly casting aside the blue overalls of her oppression and undressing for the titillated gaze of Winston, accentuates her natural beauty, and is comprehensible and symbolically explicable when situated within the context of Winston's romanticised vision of the undulating countryside as wild, untamed and sensual.

This prohibited act of sexual congress may be dangerous, but it is also a commitment that both Julia and Winston make to maintain their humanity in the face of INGSOC's oppression. And yet, this irrepressible urge to express truthfully, honestly and unequivocally an authentic sense of self – demonstrable through the twosome's relationship and Winston's writings in his diary – is juxtaposed the myriad betrayals that poison life and corrupt personal relationships in Orwell's nightmare of *Nineteen Eighty-Four*. It is true that the elderly junk shop keeper's treachery sends Winston and Julia to their fate. But Winston, who is often characterised as a hero in literary discourses, has learned that to survive he has little choice but to repress his true feelings and to present a charade to others.

For example, an early scene takes us into the heart of Winston's working life in the Ministry of Truth. At first, Winston appears to be the very image of a conscientious academic, perhaps engaged in archival work. However, we soon learn that Winston is *not* producing new knowledge: he is, instead, an enemy of truth and knowledge, a state-sponsored intellectual saboteur who, with each document that he commits to the flames, seeks to destroy the past for the benefit of his masters. Thus, his civilised and scholarly demeanour is entirely deceptive and a betrayal of the truth: in short, a visual red herring. Moreover, Winston's misleading appearance is the outer reflection of a false, pre-assigned social persona, a superficial front that masks his true identity. His life represents little more than the rehearsal and recapitulation of an illusory social role that he plays out each day at work – amounting to a betrayal of his authentic self.

Every conversation that Winston conducts with another person – apart from Julia – is couched in a devastating betrayal of the natural, but tacit, assumption that people present themselves honestly and speak openly with one another. At the beginning of the film Winston fully expects that chocolate rations will be increased because his work in the Ministry of Truth permits him access to a very limited degree of insider information. But he is circumspect and he does not divulge this to the chipper Parsons, who innocently brings it up in conversation.

Winston also lies outright to both Parsons and Syme about not having access to razors, although we later discover that he is obtaining them from the old junk shop in the prole sector. In scenes clearly redolent of Stalin's 'great purges',[9] whilst working in his 'job', Winston also realises that Syme is about to be 'vaporised' but he watches on helplessly, unable to forewarn the blissfully ignorant man of his impending doom. Winston's betrayal of the truth is also exemplified when he is instructed to expunge from history the honourable achievements of an august member of the Inner Party, Rutherford, and to attribute his accomplishments to a dead solider, Ogolvie. When walking home from work soon after, Winston peers through the window of the Chestnut Tree café. The image of a tear-stained Rutherford watching a recording of his own confession ominously – and precisely – anticipates Winston's own pathetic demise.

Throughout Radford's film, Winston is tormented by a painful and nightmarish childhood memory that he cannot seem to come to terms with. Winston remembers himself as a young boy running through the streets of a war-torn city. We later discover that Winston 'stole' a chocolate bar from the clutches of his sister whilst his mother was holding the young girl. He then ran away to eat the confectionary. When he returns, he remembers how his mother and sister had disappeared, presumed dead, and in their place the orphaned Winston was confronted by a swarm of rats. In another memory, which manifests itself as a nightmare, the young boy sees the dead body of his mother lying in the long grass. This time the rats are crawling over her corpse and O'Brien seems to be comforting the child by placing a hand on his shoulder.

As Winston relives these horrors, the distinction between reality and fantasy collapses. Perhaps his mother and sister were abducted and killed by a death squad when he was absent, but that isn't necessarily the case. What is significant is that Winston has not been able to process the pain and trauma of his mother and his sister's loss and, perhaps in response to this, he has taught himself to carry the guilty burden of their death. To a rational outsider, the notion that an innocent, starving, impoverished, defenceless young boy, who was simply a tragic victim of circumstance, could be responsible for the death of his own family is palpably absurd. For it is *Winston* who was brutally and unforgivably betrayed by the adult world he should have been able to trust. He did not steal the chocolate bar, he took it out of desperation. However, to bear some responsibility for the death of his mother and sister also permits Winston some existential[10] control over the outcome. The naive assumption that had he not stolen the chocolate bar his mother and sister might have lived, and that Winston himself would not have been killed, is suggestive of an omnipotent phantasy[11] that – no matter what – the individual always carries some degree of responsibility for what comes to pass.

But, in the end, Radford's film juxtaposes Winston's bitterly tragic and entirely misplaced feeling that he let down his mother and sister with the very *real* treacheries perpetrated by INGSOC. It is the *Party* that has betrayed humanity by abandoning the utopian ideals of the revolution, turning the dream of a fairer society into a totalitarian nightmare (is Stalin's betrayal of Lenin represented in the burning pictures of Goldstein?). INGSOC has subjected the people to incalculable misery and suffering by keeping them in slavery, destitution and on the brink of starvation. The interminable use of violence and war to destroy the products of working class labour is a perverted betrayal of the righteous socialist vision that all may share in, and benefit from, the bounty created by hard work.

Furthermore, it is the narcissistic and regressive INGSOC which has deceived humanity by setting out to annihilate the great intellectual, moral, ethical and epistemological achievements of history and classical civilisation. INGSOC has destroyed the incisive beauty of reason, logic and language. 'Newspeak', 'thoughtcrime' and 'doublethink' are miserable abominations that retard human intellectual development and potential, turning men and women back into frightened and child-like slaves.

THE PAST: ORANGES AND LEMONS...

The past is an extremely important theme in psychoanalysis. The purpose of psychotherapy is to educate an individual in how unconscious forces influence our response to the challenges of life and how these patterns of repressed thought and phantasy tend to emerge in childhood. Thus, in order to *understand* oneself, one must return to the past to become, in effect, an historian of the self.

Winston's decision to break a law punishable by death and keep a diary articulates his need to understand. It is an attempt to retrace the buried footsteps of the past by uncovering the history INGSOC has tried to obliterate. His aspiration is that he may learn to cut through his amnesia and ascertain who he *was* in the hope that he will discover *who* he truly is. In so doing, he yearns to strike a blow against the relentless fascism of INGSOC, reasserting a semblance of humanity and individual identity before time, inevitably, elapses. Thus, the solipsistic and introspective dramaturgical structure of *Nineteen Eighty-Four* loosely follows the pattern of a classic American film noir, where a fallen and jaded hero must solve a labyrinthine mystery, perhaps by confronting an existential crisis: typically his own neuroses and cynicism.

Therefore, Radford's artistic realisation and delineation of the prole sector seems to be informed by the aesthetic experimentalism of noir. On his many illicit voyages to this underworld of a neighbourhood, masked by expressionistic shadows, Winston glides inconspicuously through the dark, virtually incognito. Furthermore, Radford's oneiric depiction of the prole sector represents the external expression of Winston's heightened mental impressions of this urban environment.

Winston finds the siren allure of the prole sector impossible to withstand, partly because he knows that he may manifest his repressed sexual needs through random encounters with prostitutes and partly because he theorises that the proles represent humanity's last hope of emancipation from the foul despotism of the party. In the prole sector, Winston is relatively free. Moreover, evidence of the past still clings on to existence. For Winston, the junk shop is a goldmine of history, manifesting the past.

JAMES JARRETT

When the elderly man who runs the junk shop takes Winston upstairs, both reflect on a picture on a wall. It depicts the church of St Clement's, a Roman Catholic edifice of worship close to the Thames. The picture immediately stimulates Winston into recalling an old folksong, 'Oranges and Lemons', but he cannot remember all the words. Indeed, in a society so aggressively purged of all theological religion, he can barely identify this now designated 'museum' as once being a place of Christian ritual and ceremony (ironically, the only 'god' that the people were forced to worship after INGSOC's 'cultural revolution' was Big Brother). But then, this tantalising imprint of a memory, however fragmented, nevertheless remains. It connects Winston back to the past. Indeed, when reposing in bed with Julia, Winston again finds the ditty on his lips and begins to sing softly. He is shocked when Julia responds by answering the first line with the second. Smothered beneath the totalitarianism of 1984, is a past that links Winston and Julia through a dimly remembered, but shared, cultural heritage of art, literature and music. Equally, however, the audience is also conscious of the scene's tragic, dramatic irony. The apparently innocent and naive playfulness of 'Oranges and Lemons' soon descends into a darkly sinister verse evoking execution at the guillotine, anticipating Winston and Julia's physical and psychological destruction:

> Here comes a candle to light you to bed
>
> Here comes a chopper to chopper to chop off your head;
>
> The last, last, last, last, last, man's head (Taylor 1954: 4).

Winston's fondness for an apparently unimportant trinket – a glass bauble containing what seems to be a fragment of ancient coral – is a further illustration of his need to engage with history. Much like the vague remembrance of 'Oranges and Lemons', the trinket has mnemonic qualities and is of symbolic, rather than material, value. It is a piece of history that the party, in spite of its fanatical efforts, has failed to erase:

> Julia: What time do they cut the light in your flats?
>
> Winston: 23:30
>
> Julia: At the hostel it's 23
>
> Julia: *Goes to sideboard and picks up the glass bauble.* What is it?
>
> Winston: I don't know. A little chunk of history they've forgotten to alter. A message from a hundred years ago (Radford *1984*).

Winston's decoding of this enigmatic object as a 'message' is a subtle echo of his belief that his secret diary writings are a gift for future generations. And when the lovers hear a sturdy prole woman in the yard below their room singing what appears to be a haunting Celtic folksong, Winston is moved by her *acapella*, since it represents for him a romantic and idealised insight into a forgotten past. His assertion that the woman is the possessor of her own kind of beauty gently critiques Julia's simplistic denunciation of her robust figure. Indeed, Radford's image of Julia and Winston, in soft silhouette, both naked and gazing through the window in tender meditation, is redolent of the way in which a loving mother and father may gaze upon their new-born baby sleeping in its cot. Through the passionate communication of their procreative love – and Winston's exploration of the concealed past – the two have created the potential for a future. Yet, at the very moment Winston can acknowledge this achievement, he also seems to meditate somewhat philosophically on the impermanence of the present. Life is so short that effectively, at the very moment that we are born, 'we are the dead' (Radford *1984)*.

Again, this deeply profound rumination seems to assume the form of a nascent rhyme, perhaps mirroring the call and response structure of 'Oranges and Lemons'. But this time, in a cruel and ironic twist, it is the voice of Big Brother, rather than Winston's beloved Julia who responds to complete the rhyme with a black and menacing summary of the couple's catastrophic circumstances, telling them that it is now '*You* who are the dead'. Radford conveys the terrifying humiliation of being naked and at the mercy of INGSOC soldiers whilst also emphasising the figurative significance of the encounter. A paramilitary goon viciously punches Julia in the stomach, an act of despicable violence that demonstrates the party's pathetic hatred and fear of Julia's natural beauty and femininity, her power as a woman of childbearing age and the precious love and potential that she and Winston have created with their bodies. Winston, who is powerless in the face of this assault, watches as his glass bauble is smashed, signifying the demolition of his dream to uncover the past, any hopes that he may have for the future and the impending destruction of his fragile body and mind.

Before long, O'Brien's betrayal of Winston plays out in some of the most disturbing, graphic and realistic images of torture ever committed to film. Here Radford challenges the audience to face the horror and misery of totalitarianism by training the camera on Winston's agonised face in a series of uncompromising close-ups. However, amazingly, the agony that O'Brien inflicts through his use of the excruciating 'rack', administered with a medieval brutality that mocks INGSOC propaganda portraying Oceania as a modern, civilised and progressive society, is perhaps less painful than the psychological misery Winston is forced to endure. O'Brien's foul claim that he is trying to 'cure' Winston is not only a blatant lie, it is also a perverted inversion of the humanitarian logic behind a compassionate psychotherapeutic encounter.

The devious O'Brien intuits that Winston is seeking help, the help that he needs to be truly well, truly healthy. One particular frame, which shows O'Brien and the shattered Winston staring into a

PAPER

JAMES JARRETT

mirror manifests a gruesomely tragic parody of a psychoanalytic session where both therapist and patient stand adjacent to one another in an attempt to embody their therapeutic alliance and, poetically, to gaze out on to the patient's past as he constructs his psychobiography. Furthermore, intriguingly, O'Brien's description of Winston as 'the last man' is not only a grotesque and absurd echo of Nietzsche, it also, once again, evokes the dark and sinister ending of 'Oranges and Lemons':

The last, last, last, last, last man's head (Taylor 1954: 4).

In the end, O'Brien infects Winston's mind with his absurd and nightmarish matrix of twisted logic by inducing brute terror. Here, Radford's use of a succession of extreme close-ups of Winston trapped in the mask, the rat's twitching snout and Julia, who suddenly appears beside O'Brien as a hallucination, is a fittingly dreadful conclusion to a gruelling sequence of visceral cinematic images.

But Radford's depiction of Winston's final predicament is controversial. We see Winston sitting silently in the Chestnut Tree café, his face apparently devoid of emotion, playing chess on his own. On the screen we hear of Oceania's latest 'victory' over Eastasia and Winston's 'confession' is broadcast on a big screen. In this sequence, we see him stare dispassionately into the camera before telling the viewers of his multitude of crimes, including sabotage, visiting the prole sector and spreading venereal disease.

But as she hurries past in the grey, decimated street outside, Julia suddenly spies Winston. Risking all, she enters and tries to engage him in conversation, only to be confronted by a diminished figure who appears to be little more than a shell of a human being. However, Radford *seems to imply* that – whatever horrors O'Brien has inflicted on Winston – he still has not fully succeeded in destroying his victim's humanity. During his stilted interaction with Julia, the camera lingers on Winston's hand as he moves the pieces strategically around the board; and, although he seems to be referring to the war in Eastasia when he speculates on how 'they' might be 'outflanked', Radford seems to intimate that Winston is, in fact, making a veiled, surreptitious reference to INGSOC and attempting to tell Julia that the war with the Party for his mind and soul is still raging, silently, within. This notion – that Winston has, in fact, on some level at least, won because the Party has failed in their attempt to completely hollow him out and fill him with love for Big Brother – is indicated in Winston's failure to scratch into the dust an equation that he *still* clearly cannot accept to be true ($2+2=5$) his consent to converse with his erstwhile lover and, most poignantly, his reaction to being confronted by the face of Big Brother, as it looms over him in the café. When gazing upon the face of the tyrant he turns away and looks outside towards the street, apparently searching in his mind for Julia. The camera focuses on his tear-soaked face as he seems to whisper, under his breath: 'I'd have loved you'.

CONCLUSION

Radford's adaptation represents a concerted and significant attempt to translate Orwell's novel into the medium of moving images and is successful in capturing the atmosphere and essence of *Nineteen Eighty-Four*. Radford and his production team provide a substantial level of accurate visual, chronological and literary detail, while John Hurt and Suzanna Hamilton, as Smith and Julia respectively, produce convincing and subtle performances that contribute to the overall effectiveness of the film. However, Radford's decision to end the film by appearing to ascribe to Winston a silent rebelliousness that lurks within and manifests as an enduring love for Julia raises important ethical and moral questions pertaining to the role and function of those adapting novels for the screen. In Orwell's novel, Winston's transformation into an empty, unthinking automaton filled completely with love for the Party and hatred of its enemies seems complete. O'Brien has triumphed because now, Winston loves 'Big Brother'. But, Hurt's gaunt face does seem to have left within it some life, some humanity and some genuine love for Julia, however well he conceals it.

Perhaps, ultimately, Radford's final depiction of Winston is less a personal attempt to overlay any interpretive prejudices on *Nineteen Eighty-Four*. What Radford demonstrates, perhaps unwittingly, is how and why INGSOC's attempt to crush humanity by controlling hearts and minds must fail in the end. Winston has been successfully brainwashed by the Party: that much is true; and he has been enslaved because his mind has been reprogrammed to operate through 'doublethink'. But, history shows that systems based on illogical nonsense, fear and repression do not last indefinitely. The spirit of conscious and unconscious human love, and our need to search for freedom, reason, logic and truth will endure, even in the face of our most fearful nightmares.

NOTES

[1] A term used by psychoanalysts to describe how memories, thoughts and feelings emerge in relation to one another, not necessarily in chronological order. See Pick p.23

[2] 'Magic thinking' is a term used in psychology and psychoanalysis to refer to the belief that one can achieve a desired outcome simply by wishing it to be so. See De Mijolla p.1000

[3] An agricultural strategy for cultivating mushrooms that has now entered our common parlance to describe disingenuous ways of controlling people through misdirection and ignorance

[4] I am referring to Beckett's *Waiting for Godot*

[5] In reference to Nietzsche's concept of the 'superman' or 'overman'. See *Thus Spake Zarathustra* p. 8

[6] Sophocles was a leading figure in the tragedian culture of ancient Athens. See Beer (2004) for a comprehensive discussion of Sophocles' reputation and contribution

[7] British colloquial way for describing betrayal

[8] Infantile phantasies of a 'primal scene' play an important role in Kleinian psychoanalysis. See *Selected Melanie Klein* p. 12

[9] The great purge of Stalin, 1936-1938. Sometimes referred to as the 'great terror'

[10] In reference to Heidegger's existentialism, McGrath offers a straightforward explanation of how existentialism emerged in its historical context p. 7

[11] Concept in psychoanalysis that explains an unconscious phantasy of being 'all powerful', a defence against anxiety. Closely linked to 'magical thinking'. See De Mijolla p. 822

REFERENCES

Anderson, M. (1956) *1984:* Holiday Film Productions Ltd

Beckett, S. (1956) *Waiting For Godot*, London: Faber and Faber

Beer, J. (2004) *Sophocles and the Tragedy of Athenian Democracy*, West Port: Praeger

Bruno, U. A. (2007) *Stalin: The Man and his Era*, London: Tauris Parke Paperbacks

De Mijolla, A. (ed.) (2005) *International Dictionary of Psychoanalysis*, Detroit: Thomson Gale

Hawkes, T. (1977) *Structuralism and Semiotics*, Los Angeles: University of California Press

Luhr, W. (2012) *Film Noir*, Chichester: Wiley-Blackwell

McGrath, S. J. (2008) *Heidegger: A (Very) Critical Introduction*, Cambridge: William B. Eardman's Publishing Company

Mitchell, J. (ed.) (1986) *Selected Melanie Klein*, New York: The Free Press

Nietzsche, F. (2003 [1883]) *Thus Spake Zarathustra*, New York: Algora Publishing

Pick, D. (2015) *Psychoanalysis: A Very Short Introduction*, Oxford: Oxford University Press

Radford, M. (1984) *1984*, London: Virgin Films/Umbrella-Rosunblum Films

Taylor, G. (1954) *The Rhymes and the Churches*, London: Peter Neville

NOTE ON THE CONTRIBUTOR

James Jarrett was educated at De Montfort University, Cardiff University and Essex University. He was awarded a PhD for research in contemporary theatre and psychoanalysis under the supervision of Professor Jonathan Lichtenstein. He worked as a performer before returning to education to lecture in theatre and the performing arts. He has taught at Essex University and at University Centre Colchester where, as course leader, he authored the innovative BA Honours Degree programme in Acting. He has presented papers on theatre, performance, acting and culture to conferences at Essex, Bristol and Middlesex Universities.

PAPER

The Politics of the Uncanny: George Orwell and the Paranormal

PHILIP BOUNDS

This paper examines George Orwell's scattered writings on the paranormal. It argues that Orwell's approach to the strange world of poltergeists, mediumship and precognition was powerfully influenced by his political concerns. On the one hand, he seemed to believe that paranormal beliefs and practices often reflected the warped psychology of the totalitarian age. On the other hand – notably in Nineteen Eighty-Four *– he wrote about the paranormal in a more positive register and implied that it could sometimes have politically progressive consequences. Taken as a whole, Orwell's writings on the paranormal provide us with a more nuanced understanding of his spiritual beliefs.*

Keywords: Orwell, paranormal, totalitarianism, *Nineteen Eighty-Four*

PERSONAL EXPERIENCES

As with most people, Orwell's interest in the paranormal grew out of his personal experience of apparently inexplicable events. The most disconcerting of these occurred during his first year at Eton. Appalled by the rough treatment meted out to new boys by members of the elite College Sixth Form, Orwell conceived a particular dislike for a sixth-former called Philip Yorke. He and his friend Steven Runciman sought revenge on their oppressor by making a crude effigy of Yorke and inflicting symbolic punishment on it. Orwell suggested driving a pin through the effigy's torso, but Runciman persuaded him to adopt the more moderate tactic of breaking off one of its legs. Not long afterwards, Yorke duly broke a leg. Shortly after that he died of leukaemia. Orwell and Runciman were both mortified.[1] As Gordon Bowker has pointed out, Orwell's foray into do-it-yourself occultism might well have reinforced some of the most salient aspects of his emerging personality. Already an outsider and unreasonably anxious about his perceived lack of moral fibre, he probably regarded Yorke's death as further evidence of his own turpitude: 'No doubt the belief that he had caused a death left him feeling even more isolated and different, and fearful of the damage he could cause others' (Bowker 2003: 56).

PHILIP BOUNDS Orwell's next recorded brush with the paranormal occurred at the start of one of his most famous tramping expeditions. Towards the end of August 1931, Orwell set out from his parents' house in Southwold to go hop-picking in the fields of Kent. (The trip was later written up in his so-called 'Hop-Picking Diary' and provided the inspiration for some of the central chapters in *A Clergyman's Daughter*.)[2] A mere two days into his travels, while resting outside Walberswick Church in Suffolk, he claimed to have seen a ghost. Describing the sighting in a vivid letter to his friend Dennis Collings, Orwell said that he had glanced over his shoulder and seen 'a figure ... disappearing behind the masonry & presumably entering the churchyard' (Collings 1931b: 211). Although he cast no more than a casual glance at it, he got the distinct impression that it was 'a man's figure, small & stooping, & dressed in lightish brown; I should have said a workman' (Orwell 1931b: 211). Then, suddenly realising that it had made no sound, he decided to follow it:

> There was no one in the churchyard, & no one within possible distance along the road – this was about 20 seconds after I had seen it ... I looked into the church. The only people there were the vicar, dressed in *black*, & a workman who, as far as I remember, had been sawing the whole time ... The figure had therefore vanished (ibid: 211).

Orwell's response to this experience was by no means entirely credulous. Indeed, his laconic interpretation of what happened shows that he refused to think of the ghost in straightforwardly supernatural terms: 'Presumably an hallucination' (ibid).[3] Nevertheless, the letter to Collings provides a fascinating insight into the religious pressures to which Orwell's mind was prey. Despite admitting that he only saw the putative ghost out of the corner of his eye – and even though its apparent disappearance can be explained in all kinds of non-paranormal ways – Orwell seemed curiously adamant that he had experienced something out of the ordinary. The possibility that he had not seen a ghost at all seems not to have occurred to him. It was as if a suppressed yearning for the numinous had temporarily transformed the bluff, empirically-minded Englishman into someone for whom evidence was less importance than the need to believe.

It also seems significant that the letter to Collings segues from a discussion of the paranormal into a staunch defence of Protestantism. Describing a virulently anti-Catholic advertisement in the window of a shop owned by the Bible Society, Orwell gives a tongue-in-cheek endorsement of its spirit of Protestant militancy: 'Long may they fight, I say; so long as that spirit is in the land we are safe from the RCs' (ibid: 212). Perhaps he was implying that the average Catholic was too spiritually insensitive – too weighed down by a prosaic belief in justification through good works – to entertain an open-minded interest in ghosts and other aspects of the paranormal. If so, his argument was no less unfair than some of the anti-Catholic points in his later works.

SITWELL AND POLTERGEISTS

Orwell's personal experience of the paranormal fed through into his work as a book reviewer, essayist and novelist. Two of his book reviews provide especially interesting evidence of the way his thinking about the paranormal intersected with his wider beliefs. The first – a brief survey of Sacheverell Sitwell's *Poltergeists* – appeared in *Horizon* in September 1940. Sitwell's book, which drew on material dating as far back as the seventeenth century, combined a lengthy commentary by its author with excerpts from ten existing works on noteworthy poltergeists. It cannot be said that Orwell's review of it was entirely accurate. While rightly noting that Sitwell rejected the idea that poltergeist activity is caused by the discarnate spirits of the dead, he also claimed that Sitwell believed that every last instance of it is 'due to human trickery, conscious and unconscious' (Orwell 1940a: 247). This clearly conflicted with Sitwell's belief that many poltergeists involve human agents exercising authentically paranormal powers: 'Making allowance, a thousand times over for exaggeration, something must remain' (Sitwell 1940: 38).

However, Orwell was much more acute when he commented on the relevance of poltergeists to our understanding of human nature. Working on the assumption that all poltergeist activity is caused by human beings, he was palpably dismayed by the extreme vindictiveness which appeared to underscore it. He clearly found it astonishing that an individual could go to such extraordinary lengths to terrify other members of his own family, noting that 'Why they do it, what pleasure they get out of it, is completely unknown' (Orwell 1940a: 247). There are clear echoes here of the profoundly disenchanted vision of human nature which found its ultimate expression in the pages of *Nineteen Eighty-Four*. Orwell's implied argument is that there is no real difference between the adolescent mischief-makers who simulate poltergeists and the power-hungry bureaucrats who impose totalitarian rule on their fellow human beings. Each of them is driven by a hunger to exercise power *for its own sake*. There is also a case for saying that Orwell's comments on *Poltergeists* reflected his despair at the corruption of the family unit in the totalitarian age. As a number of scenes in *Nineteen Eighty-Four* go to show, Orwell knew that dictatorships of the left and right had often managed to destroy family loyalties by encouraging children to denounce their parents for political heresy (see, for example, Orwell 2000 [1949]: 24n). Perhaps, at some level of his mind, he saw the teenage poltergeist as a sort of supernatural antecedent for the ultra-zealous member of the Oceanian Youth League.

PHILIP BOUNDS One of the poltergeists to which Sitwell drew attention occurred in Connecticut in the home of the Rev. Eliakim Phelps between March 1850 and October 1851 (Sitwell 1940: 45n). Among its most unusual features was the appearance of what Sitwell called 'tableaux'. After arriving home from church on the morning of 10 March 1850, the Phelps family discovered eleven elaborately dressed dolls in their dining room. The dolls had been arranged in such a way as to present a spectacle of extreme piety: most of them were at prayer, though one of them hovered above the rest as if levitating. At the heart of the group was 'the figure of a dwarf grotesquely dressed' (ibid: 46). Approximately twenty more figures were to appear before the poltergeist activity came to an end. Sitwell rejected any supernatural explanation for this strange proliferation of dolls. His best guess was that they had all been produced by the Rev. Phelps's sixteen-year-old daughter. More precisely, he argued that this whole episode 'would seem to be a perversion of the children's game of dressing dolls' (ibid: 53). In giving vent to a species of spiritual extremism, Phelps's daughter was effectively subverting the religious impulse by imbuing it with an element of the grotesque. In that respect – or so Sitwell pointed out – her behaviour was comparable to that of the medieval nuns who dressed the bones of saints in 'court clothes … crowns and diadems' (ibid: 54).

Orwell made no reference to the so-called 'Phelps case' in his review of *Poltergeists*, but he raised the matter with Sitwell in a letter he wrote to him on 6 July 1940. Harking back to the period in the early 1930s when he lived in Southwold and served as a tutor to a young boy called Bryan Morgan, Orwell recalled his own haunting encounter with an instance of the eccentric use of dolls' clothes. One day, while walking across Walberswick Common, Orwell and Morgan came across a parcel that had been abandoned under a gorse bush. What they found when they unwrapped it was understatedly described by Orwell as 'something vaguely unwholesome':

> It was a cardboard box about 10" by 6" by 3" deep. Inside we found that it was lined with cloth and made up like a little room, with tiny furniture made of matchwood and scraps of cloth glued together. There were also … some tiny female garments including underclothes. There was also a scrap of paper with 'This is not bad is it?' (or nearly those words) written on it in an evidently feminine hand (Orwell 1940b: 208-209).

Unlike Sitwell, Orwell was not inclined to explain the misuse of dolls' clothes in religious terms. Instead, he expressed the view that the box on Walberswick Common had been 'made by someone suffering from some kind of sexual aberration' (ibid: 209). Here, too, one catches an echo of his wider anxieties about the degeneration of human nature in a totalitarian age. As his depiction of the relationship between Winston and Julia in *Nineteen Eighty-Four* serves to illustrate, Orwell was fascinated by the politics of sexuality. Indeed, there was more than a hint of a sort of plain man's Reich or Marcuse about him. Convinced that sexuality in its natural, uninhibited and uncorrupted form could endow the individual with deep feelings of autonomy, he clearly regarded erotic fulfilment as a valuable undergirding for democratic culture and a powerful specific against authoritarianism. The obverse side of his faith in sexuality was a deep anxiety about the forces seeking to subvert it. His writings are full of examples of the erotic impulse being corrupted by the exigencies of power. Totalitarian governments, American detective fiction, soulless holiday camps – Orwell believed that these and many other things were prompting people to think of sexuality as a means of domination.

It is clear from the letter to Sitwell that he regarded the paranormal as yet another site of this corrupting influence. In his implied reinterpretation of the Phelps case (as well as in his comments on the Walberswick parcel), Orwell seems to suggest that the perversion of the 'doll-dressing impulse' reflects a desire to disorientate other people through the expression of an unwholesome sexual sensibility. The fact that the dolls had been dressed by young women probably struck him as especially sinister. Largely uncritical in his attitude towards prevailing gender stereotypes, Orwell clearly regarded women as the guardians of authentic sexuality. Any evidence that they had deviated from the true path of sexual virtue tended to disquiet him.

DANIEL DUNGLAS HOME AND MEDIUMSHIP

The second of Orwell's book reviews to deal with paranormal themes appeared in the *Observer* on 6 June 1948. The text under review was Jean Burton's *Heyday of a Wizard*, a biography of the Victorian medium Daniel Dunglas Home (Burton 1948). Although Home is now primarily known only to parapsychologists and aficionados of the occult, he was widely fêted across Europe and the USA in the thirty or so years before his death in 1886. At his innumerable séances – most of them held in clear light and often attended by leading writers, scientists and society figures – he produced some of the most dramatic instances on record of what parapsychologists call 'physical phenomena'. Musical instruments played without being touched. Heavy tables rose into the air. Mysterious hands materialised out of nowhere and presented flowers to the sitters. On one occasion, Home appeared to float out of a third-floor window and then float back in through an adjacent one. (Orwell wryly described this incident as 'very justly celebrated if it really happened' (Orwell 1948: 389).) On no occasion was he plausibly accused of cheating.[4]

PHILIP BOUNDS Orwell's assessment of Home was at once scrupulously fair-minded and resolutely sceptical. Emphasising the fact that Home had never been detected doing anything dishonest, he dismissed the idea that he could simply be regarded as a 'conscious fraud'. On the other hand, he gave short shrift to the claim that Home's abilities were authentically paranormal. There are times in his review of Burton's book when his suspicion of the paranormal seems well-nigh Humean in its dogmatic materialism. He refuses to believe *on principle* that the mind can ever subvert the laws of nature and directly affect the behaviour of the material world:

> And yet – a point that Miss Jean Burton fails to emphasise – there must have been imposture of some kind. Many of the stories that are told of Home are flatly incredible. ... It is clear that things of this kind cannot actually have happened (Orwell 1948: 388-389).

If Home was not the genuine medium he claimed to be, how did he manage to convince so many eminent people that his spectacular séance performances were entirely authentic? Orwell's answer to that question once again intersects with his political concerns. Echoing the argument of the early psychic investigator Frank Podmore, he suggested that Home must have induced his sitters into seeing impossible things by hypnotising them at the start of his performances. (Interestingly, Orwell acknowledged that Home's hypnotic gift may have been 'unconscious'. He was not necessarily accusing him of out-and-out deception.)[5] It is hard to read Orwell's account of Home engendering 'delusions in whole groups of people' without being reminded of an early description of a Big Brother poster in *Nineteen Eighty-Four*: 'The black moustachio'd face gazed down from every commanding corner ... the dark eyes looked deep into Winston's own' (Orwell 2000 [1949]: 4). In the age of Hitler, Stalin and Mussolini, Orwell had an almost hypersensitive fear of the capacity of charismatic leaders to subject ordinary people to a kind of political hypnosis. For all his evident affection for Home, he perhaps perceived an analogy between his alleged hypnotic gifts and the more mind-warping aspects of totalitarian statecraft. Capacities put to relatively innocuous uses in the séance room could sometimes be used to enslave entire peoples, or so Orwell implied.[6]

YEATS, FASCISM AND THE OCCULT

There was nothing explicitly political about Orwell's reviews of *Poltergeists* and *Heyday of a Wizard*. Their observations about human nature and the techniques of mass persuasion were not directly linked to their author's wider concerns about the totalitarian age. It was only in his great essay on W. B. Yeats that Orwell's understanding of the relationship between politics and the paranormal came into explicit focus. Although many of the leading British modernists had an interest in the occult, Yeats was the only one who used occult doctrine as the basis of his work. Having absorbed a range of esoteric ideas while serving as a highly credulous member of the Order of the Golden Dawn, he ended up expounding an idiosyncratic magical doctrine of his own in his book *A Vision* (1925). The book cast considerable retrospective light on his poetry, making it clear that its themes, forms and techniques had been shaped by occult doctrine all along.[7] At the same time, Yeats had a long history of involvement with the politics of the authoritarian right. Inclined to idealise the Irish Protestant aristocracy from which his family hailed, he cherished the idea of an anti-democratic Irish republic in which a deferential peasantry would submit to the rule of people like himself. By the early 1930s, frustrated by the decidedly non-Protestant orientation of the newly independent Eire, he briefly became a supporter of the fascist Blueshirt movement. Scholars and critics have debated the extent of his commitment to fascism ever since.[8]

Orwell's essay on Yeats appeared in *Horizon* in January 1943 and took the form of a response to V. K. Narayana Menon's *The Development of William Butler Yeats* (1942). Its chief purpose was to explore the relationship between the political and the metaphysical elements of Yeats's work. Why was a supporter of the authoritarian right so attracted to occult ideas? In seeking to answer that question, Orwell was not simply contributing to the debate about a particular poet. Given that a fascination with the occult had been a recurring characteristic of fascist cultural politics, he was also trying to deepen his readers' understanding of one of the most arcane but potent elements in the outlook of an entire political movement. His main argument was that fascism and occultism were bound together by their elitism and their shared belief in the cyclical nature of history. At a very simple level, the fascist faith in the rule of elites – the adamantine belief of people like Hitler and Mussolini that ordinary people were incapable of running their own affairs – chimed with the occult belief that only the gifted few could achieve the status of magical initiates. According to Orwell, one of the components of this elitist perspective was the conviction that 'knowledge must be a secret thing' (Orwell 1943a: 282). Just as the devotee of the occult prides themselves on their mastery of secret doctrines, so the fascist regards ideology as something which should only circulate among the intellectual caste.

Closely linked to this emphasis on elitism is the belief in what Orwell called 'our old friend, the cyclical universe, in which everything happens over and over again' (Orwell 1943a: 281). Writing at a time when many intellectuals believed that history was moving in a broadly linear fashion towards the establishment of an egalitarian utopia, Orwell pointed out that a cyclical view of history brought immense solace to anyone who hated the idea of equality. If human

PAPER

societies are destined to repeat all the stages of their historical development, it follows that the age of liberty, equality and fraternity will rapidly revert to the more time-honoured principles of discipline, hierarchy and charity:[9] 'It does not much matter if the lower orders are getting above themselves, for, after all, we shall soon be returning to an age of tyranny' (ibid). In a throwaway line, Orwell also suggested that fascism and occultism shared a 'profound hostility ... to the Christian ethical code' (ibid). What he presumably meant by this was that both ideologies aspired to achieve a sort of Nietzschean transvaluation of values, seeking to realise their goals by moving beyond existing distinctions between good and evil.

Orwell's comments ignored the rich body of occult doctrine which takes an explicitly Christian form. The essay on Yeats makes it clear that Orwell regarded occult doctrine as inherently sinister. On the other hand, in an interestingly self-revealing aside, he resisted the idea that Yeats should be condemned outright for embracing the occult perspective. The reason for his comparative tolerance was that there was no Chinese wall dividing Yeats from all the rest of us: 'I believe it could be shown that *some* degree of belief in magic is almost universal' (ibid: 281). Elsewhere, in a separate review of Narayana Menon's book, Orwell even went so far as to cite Yeats's occultism as an instance of what made contemporary literary culture tick. Pointing out that sincerity was the *sine qua non* of literary excellence in post-Renaissance societies, Orwell argued that the magnificence of Yeats's work was a testament to what writers were capable of when they strove to express their most deeply cherished beliefs:

> ... for a writer, common sense matters less than sincerity. ... Yeats may have held some absurd or undesirable beliefs, and he may have laid claim to a mystic wisdom that he did not possess, but he would never in any circumstances have committed what he would have regarded as an aesthetic sin (Orwell 1943b: 71).

The irony here was rich. When Orwell tried to explain why totalitarianism posed such a grave threat to literary culture, he claimed that its collectivist ethos subverted the emphasis on individual sincerity which had underpinned all the great works of the modern age. No writer could produce valuable work if he suppressed his own beliefs in order to express the perspective of an authoritarian regime.[10] By invoking Yeats to illustrate the necessity of individual sincerity, Orwell was implying that he (Yeats) would have been one of the first people to suffer if the right-wing movements he supported ever came to power. Yeats was too much of an individualist to thrive in an authoritarian age. The fascism to which he gave cautious allegiance would have been the end of him as a writer.

PRECOGNITION AS A SUBVERSIVE FORCE

Orwell's perspective on the paranormal in his writings on poltergeists, mediumship and fascism was unremittingly bleak. Nevertheless, as his letter to Dennis Collings reminds us, there were times when he seemed amused by manifestations of the paranormal and refused to see them as necessarily sinister.[11] This more positive strain in his thinking received its most powerful expression in *Nineteen Eighty-Four*. Although one can scarcely claim that Orwell's final novel was steeped in supernatural concerns, one of its implied arguments is among the most startling in the Orwellian oeuvre: precognition is not merely a reality but also a powerful antidote to the totalitarian world view.

Nineteen Eighty-Four's engagement with the theme of precognition is woven into its portrait of the relationship between Winston and O'Brien. Some twenty pages into the text, Winston recalls a haunting dream from a few years earlier. While making his way through a room entirely devoid of light, the dreaming Winston had heard a voice telling him that 'We shall meet in the place where there is no darkness' (Orwell 2000 [1949]: 27). A little while later he realises that the voice was that of O'Brien, a member of the Inner Party to whom he feels powerfully drawn. The precognitive status of the dream only becomes clear when Winston is arrested and taken to the Ministry of Love for interrogation. Not only are all the rooms in the Ministry permanently illuminated by a harsh and unforgiving light but O'Brien himself is Winston's chief interrogator. Winston's dream – to which he had not ascribed any sinister connotation – accurately predicted the circumstances in which his punishment for dissidence would begin.

Why did Orwell include a precognitive dream in his final novel? It would be a mistake to see it simply as a means of building a sense of suspense. Its real significance is only laid bare when O'Brien speaks to Winston about the philosophical outlook of the totalitarian state. As Winston knows only too well from his work at the Ministry of Truth, total dictatorships of the Oceanian variety put a premium on the thoroughgoing manipulation of reality. It is not simply that the powers that be lie continuously about their actions in the present. Equally fundamental is their manipulation of the historical records to ensure that there is no perception of inconsistency between the Party's current position and its behaviour in the past. The obsessive rewriting of newspapers and other sources of historical information is one of the central means by which the obedience of the masses is secured. When O'Brien speaks to Winston about the nature of the Oceanian power structures, he makes it clear that the Party's instinctive mendacity – its shameless belief that every last event in the past, present and future should be distorted for political ends – necessarily implies an extreme form of philosophical idealism. In order to justify their tampering with reality, Party intellectuals cling

> Only the disciplined mind can see reality, Winston. You believe that reality is something objective, external, existing in its own right. ... But I tell you, Winston, that reality is not external. Reality exists in the human mind, and nowhere else. Not in the individual mind, which can make mistakes, and in any case soon perishes: only in the mind of the Party, which is collective and immortal. Whatever the Party holds to be truth, *is* truth (ibid: 261).

O'Brien's startling philosophical disquisition throws the subversive power of Winston's precognitive dream into vivid relief. By collapsing the distinction between reality and the will of the Party, O'Brien is effectively saying that no event can ever be regarded as fixed for all eternity. The only thing the Party has to do to effect a change to the historical record is to exercise its collective intelligence. Orwell's implied point is that precognition poses a clear challenge to this politically charged version of Berkeleyan idealism. If it is possible to see into the future, it arguably follows that certain events occur *necessarily*. Some aspects of the future are fixed in advance and no amount of political tampering can ever alter them. Totalitarian metaphysics run adrift on the rocks of clairvoyance. Orwell's emphasis on the subversive power of precognition complements his more widely recognised emphasis on the subversive power of history. One of Winston's most salient characteristics is his determination to sustain his fragile memories of what life was like before the Party came to power. Dimly remembered nursery rhymes and cheap trinkets glimpsed in antique shops illuminate his days and dreams. His preoccupation with the past is not simply a matter of nostalgia. Instead it grows out of the sense that the Party legitimises its rule by claiming that life has been infinitely better since it acquired state power. In seeking to sustain the opposite view – in continually telling himself that the Party's rise precipitated a catastrophic decline in his country's fortunes – Winston is challenging the status quo by forging the rudiments of an alternative view of history. This makes him the sort of dissident for whom the past and the future are central weapons in the struggle against an intolerable present.

CONCLUSION

No one would claim that an interest in the paranormal lies at the heart of Orwell's work. His references to ghosts, poltergeists and the like are few and far between and not always entirely well informed. Having said that, his infrequent writings on the paranormal clearly add something to our understanding of his life and work. One of the things they underscore is the sheer consistency of his intellectual concerns. The historian Maurice Cowling once observed that the great 'monuments' of liberal writing tend to 'drive a small number of ideas about thought, politics, knowledge and religion through an extraordinary range of material' (Cowling 2001: 345).[12] Orwell's writings on the paranormal suggest that Cowling had a point. Even when engaging with something as ostensibly apolitical as the world of the unexplained, Orwell instinctively sought to analyse it in political terms. Back in the 1980s, Bernard Crick hinted that admirers of Orwell can be divided into two groups. The first consists of people who primarily admire him for his political insights; the second of people who are drawn to his cultural concerns and see his politics as something of a distraction (Crick 1984: 251f). The writings surveyed in this article suggest that the members of the second group are badly mistaken. There is no clear distinction between Orwell the cultural critic and Orwell the political analyst. His work is political through and through.

More importantly, Orwell's writings on the paranormal add a nuance or two to our understanding of his spiritual perspective. As many commentators on his work have pointed out, Orwell was haunted by the decline of religious faith in modern societies.[13] Incapable of believing in God or in a life hereafter, he greatly regretted the way that secularisation had robbed humanity of one of its main sources of consolation. He also believed that what Nietzsche famously called the death of God had created the psychological preconditions for the rise of totalitarianism. In the final analysis – or so the argument goes – Orwell was one of millions of people in the twentieth century whose renunciation of the supernatural was simultaneously regretful and absolute. He simply saw no future for religion in a world dominated by rationalism. One of the most interesting things about the writings on the supernatural is that they force us to question this view of Orwell as an out-and-out unbeliever. It is not uncommon for people who lose their religious faith to take an interest in the paranormal. (Indeed, the emergence of parapsychology in its modern form can be traced to the post-Darwinian religious crisis of the nineteenth century.) No longer capable of believing in God, they still yearn for evidence that the world is not as soulless or spiritually impoverished as orthodox materialism implies. It is perhaps not too fanciful to say that Orwell belonged among their number. Although many of his comments about the paranormal were highly sceptical, others betrayed an anguished desire to believe. His evident pleasure at seeing a ghost, his belief that precognition could subvert the totalitarian state, even his desire to see his adopted son's astrological birth chart – all these things suggested a sort of post-religious need to perceive an element of cosmic order in an apparently meaningless universe.

G. K. Chesterton is often credited with saying that when man ceases to believe in God, he does not believe in nothing but in anything.[14] There were times when George Orwell came close to illustrating the truth of this dictum. In retaining a muted desire to believe in spiritual values – in always approaching the strange world

PAPER

of the paranormal with an open mind – he displayed a subtler understanding of human needs than many of his triumphantly materialist contemporaries. He knew that there was more in heaven and earth than was dreamed of in Bertrand Russell's philosophy.

NOTES

[1] The fullest account of this incident can be found in Bowker 2003: 56. Indeed, Bowker's version of the story corrects a distorted account which had been circulating since Christopher Hollis published his book on Orwell in 1956. According to Hollis – a friend of Orwell's at Eton – Orwell had fashioned an effigy of an older boy known pseudonymously as 'Jackson major' because he thought him too noisy. Jackson major was subsequently thrashed by prefects on two successive days without having done anything to deserve it. There is no reference to broken legs or premature deaths in this version of the tale. Far from being plunged into guilt, Orwell responded to the news of Jackson major's punishment with a 'smile of wry triumph'. Significantly enough, Hollis makes it clear that Jackson major had a younger brother at Eton who was a friend of Orwell's and who later became a 'scholar of world renown'. It seems likely that this was a reference to Steven Runciman and that Jackson major can therefore be identified as Runciman's brother Leslie. Whereas Bowker portrays the younger Runciman as Orwell's occult co-conspirator, Hollis relegates him to the status of a mere observer. See Hollis 1956: 12n. Hollis's version of events has been incorporated into all the major biographies of Orwell, except Bowker's. See Crick 1992 [1980]: 104-105; Shelden 1991: 65-66; Myers 2000: 33-34; Taylor 2003: 47-48

[2] See Orwell 1931a; Orwell 2000 [1935]: 85n

[3] It is a pity that Orwell did not elaborate on this statement. Was he suggesting that the ghost was simply a projection of his own unconscious mind? Or was he alluding to the idea – now widely known as the stone-tape theory – that events can somehow be imprinted on the environment in which they occur and effectively played back at a later date?

[4] There is a voluminous literature on Home. For a recent biography, see Lamont 2005

[5] Parapsychologists have tended to shy away from the idea that mediums such as Home are able to hypnotise their audiences, not least because individuals vary widely in their capacity to be hypnotised. For a concise overview of the anti-hypnosis thesis, see Braude 2016. Available online at https://psi-encyclopedia.spr.ac.uk/articles/eyewitness-testimony-analysis

[6] Orwell also made some sceptical remarks about mediumship in his 'As I Please' column in *Tribune* on 24 November 1944. His main point on this occasion was that scientists often get taken in by mediums whereas writers rarely do. See Orwell 1944a: 471

[7] There is a very large literature on Yeats's preoccupation with the occult. For an accessible introduction, see Maddox 1999

[8] For a highly readable introduction to the various positions on the issue of Yeats's relationship to fascism, see O'Brien 1994

[9] The phrase 'discipline, hierarchy, charity' was coined by the hardline French conservative thinker Charles Maurras. It is quoted in Griffiths 1978: 135

[10] Orwell wrote about the relationship between individual sincerity and modern literary culture on numerous occasions. His most substantial discussion of the relevant issues can be found in his essay 'The prevention of literature'. See Orwell 1946

[11] Another minor example of his more positive perspective on the paranormal occurred in July 1944 when he asked his friend Rayner Heppenstall to draw up an astrological birth chart for his adopted son Richard. See Orwell 1944b

[12] Cowling made this remark while discussing the work of the historian Joseph Needham

[13] See, among many examples, Thiemann 2004

[14] Chesterton never uttered the aphorism with which he is so often credited. Specialists regard it as a slightly inaccurate translation of a statement made by Émile Cammaerts in a French-language book on Chesterton

REFERENCES

Bowker, Gordon (2003) *George Orwell*, London: Little Brown

Braude, Stephen E. (2016) Eyewitness Testimony (Analysis), *Psi Encyclopedia*, London: Society for Psychical Research

Burton, Jean (1948) *Heyday of a Wizard: Daniel Home the Medium*, London: Harrap

Cowling, Maurice (2001) *Religion and Public Doctrine in Modern England, Vol. 3: Accommodations*, Cambridge: Cambridge University Press

Crick, Bernard (1984) On the Orwell trail, *Granta*, 14 pp 236-254

Crick, Bernard (1992 [1980]) *George Orwell: A Life*, Harmondsworth: Penguin

Griffiths, Richard (1978) British Conservatism and the lessons of the Continental Right, Cowling, Maurice (ed.) *Conservative Essays*, London: Cassell pp 131-140

Hollis, Christopher (1956) *A Study of George Orwell: The Man and his Works*, London: Hollis and Carter

Lamont, Peter (2005) *The First Psychic: The Peculiar Mystery of a Notorious Victorian Wizard*, London: Little, Brown

Maddox, Brenda (1999) *George's Ghost: A New Life of W. B. Yeats*, London: Picador

Meyers, Jeffrey (2000) *Orwell: Wintry Conscience of a Generation*, London: W. W. Norton

O'Brien, Conor Cruise (1994) What rough beast: Yeats and fascism, Akenson, Donald Harman (ed.) *Conor: Anthology*, Montreal: McGill Queen's University Press pp 71-84

Orwell, George (1931a) Hop-picking diaries, Davison, Peter (ed.) (2010) *Diaries*, London: Penguin Books pp 1-22

Orwell, George (1931b) To Dennis Collings, Davison, Peter (ed.) (2000) *Complete Works of George Orwell* (hereafter *CWGO*), Vol. 1, London: Secker and Warburg pp 211-212

Orwell, George (1940a) Review of *Poltergeists* by Sacheverell Sitwell, *Horizon*, September, Davison, Peter (ed.) (2000) *CWGO*, Vol. VII, London: Secker and Warburg pp 246-248

Orwell, George (1940b) To Sacheverell Sitwell, Davison, Peter (ed.) (2000) *CWGO*, Vol. VII, London: Secker and Warburg pp 208-209

Orwell, George (1943a) Review of *The Development of W. B. Yeats* by R.K. Narayana Menon, *Horizon*, September, Davison, Peter (ed.) (2001) *CWGO*, Vol. XIV, London: Secker and Warburg pp 279-283

Orwell, George (1943b) Review of *The Development of W. B. Yeats* by R.K. Narayana Menon, *Time and Tide*, 17 April, Davison, Peter (ed.) (2001) *CWGO*, Vol. XV, London: Secker and Warburg pp 69-71

Orwell, George (1944a) As I Please, 49, *Tribune*, 24 November, Davison, Peter (ed.) (2001) *CWGO*, Vol. XVI, London: Secker and Warburg pp 471-473

Orwell, George (1944b) To Rayner Heppenstall, Davison, Peter (ed.) (2001) *CWGO*, Vol. XVI, London: Secker and Warburg p. 295

Orwell, George (1946) The prevention of literature, *Polemic*, January, Davison, Peter (ed.) (2001) *CWGO*, Vol. XVII, London: Secker and Warburg pp 369-381

Orwell, George (1948) Review of *Heyday of a Wizard* by Jean Burton, *Observer*, 6 June 1948, Davison, Peter (ed.) (2002) *CWGO*, Vol. XIX, London: Secker and Warburg pp 388-390

Orwell, George (2000 [1949]) *Nineteen Eighty-Four*, London: Penguin

Orwell, George (2000 [1935]) *A Clergyman's Daughter*, London: Penguin

Shelden, Michael (1991) *Orwell: The Authorised Biography*, London: Heinemann

Sitwell, Sacheverell (1940) *Poltergeists: An Introduction and Examination followed by Chosen Instances*, London: Faber and Faber

Taylor, D. J. (2003) *Orwell: The Life*, London: Chatto and Windus

Thiemann, Ronald F. (2004), The public intellectual as connected critic: George Orwell and religion, Cushman, Thomas and Rodden, John (eds) *George Orwell into the Twenty-First Century*, London: Paradigm Publishers pp 96-110

NOTE ON THE CONTRIBUTOR

Philip Bounds is a historian, journalist and critic. He holds a PhD in Politics from the University of Wales and is the author of a number of books, including *Orwell and Marxism* (2009), *British Communism and the Politics of Literature* (2012) and *Notes from the End of History* (2014).

PAPER

Nineteen Eighty-Four, the Secret State and the Julia Conundrum

RICHARD LANCE KEEBLE

Julia, the 'girl from the English Department' with whom Winston Smith conducts a passionate affair in Nineteen Eighty-Four, *remains one of the novel's most intriguing characters. This paper argues that her place in the novel is understandable only in the context of Orwell's complex relationship with Britain's intelligence services. It will explore the various ways in which Julia has been interpreted – by both feminists and (mainly male) Orwellian biographers – and how her representation is part of a more general discussion in the novel about sexuality. The paper will go on to present an original and critical perspective on Julia – and its epistemological implications. This interpretation helps give Orwell's celebrated dystopian novel a particularly modern character – making it essentially about the slippery, unstable nature of meaning.*

Keywords: *Nineteen Eighty-Four*, Julia, secret state, epistemology

> Secret service history may be a health hazard. It attacks the mind. In long periods immersed in it everything looks different. … There is no firm ground anywhere: no certainties, no reference points. People turn out to be not what they seemed; institutions do not function as they were supposed to; accepted truths may be deliberate disinformation; spies and moles are everywhere; and the cleverest and most dangerous of them are those who appear most unlikely and innocent.
> Bernard Porter: *Plots and Paranoia* (1989: 228)

ORWELL, ASTOR, THE SPOOKS AND THE MAKING OF *NINETEEN EIGHTY-FOUR*

It is impossible to consider the role of Julia in *Nineteen Eighty-Four* and the ways in which the novel highlights the horrors of a Big Brother surveillance society without considering the crucial role played by his friend, David Astor, in Orwell's final years.

It was Cyril Connolly who introduced Orwell to fellow old-Etonian and millionaire David Astor in 1941 – and after Orwell's

RICHARD LANCE KEEBLE

wife Eileen died suddenly in 1945, he arguably became the most important influence on his life. Indeed, following their meeting at the Langham Hotel, near Broadcasting House, where Orwell was working as a producer in the Indian Section of the BBC's Eastern Department, in 1941, the two immediately became friends (Lewis 2016: 22). Astor's family owned the *Observer;* he became its highly distinguished editor between 1948 and 1975 – and, from March 1942, Orwell made regular contributions such as profiles and book reviews to the newspaper until his death.

Significantly, Astor also introduced Orwell to the world of intelligence. Astor's intelligence ties went back as far as 1939 when he did 'secret service stuff', according to his cousin, Joyce Grenfell (Macintyre 2014: 201). Phillip Knightley records that when, in July 1939, Col. Count Gerhardt von Schwerin, of the German General Staff, arrived in the UK as a spokesman for the German opposition to Hitler, he was met by David Astor (1989: 131). He served in the early part of the Second World War in naval intelligence alongside Ian Fleming (author of the James Bond spy novels) and Dennis Wheatley (later to become the occult/adventure novelist) (see Cabell 2008: 12, 29, 49) and later with the covert Special Operations Executive (SOE).[1] Thereafter, he maintained close links with intelligence.

Astor also introduced Orwell to other intelligence friends through the Shanghai dining group (named after the Soho restaurant where they met) which he had created with his friend and Old-Harrovian Edward Hulton (Purvis and Hulbert 2016: 158). Old-Etonians in the group included Guy Burgess (later exposed as a Soviet spy), Frank Pakenham (later Lord Longford) and John Strachey.

After leaving the BBC in November 1943, Orwell planned to report for the *Observer* from Algiers and Sicily following the Allied landings but the authorities turned him down on health grounds. Orwell then quickly acquired the post of literary editor at the leftist weekly *Tribune*, which he held until February 1945 when he resigned to take on a war reporting assignment for Astor's *Observer* and the *Manchester Evening News*.[2] Was this a cover for an intelligence mission? Intriguingly, most of the men he met in Paris on his assignment – A. J. 'Freddie' Ayer, Harold Acton, Ernest Hemingway, Malcolm Muggeridge – were either Old-Etonians, working for intelligence services of one kind or another – or both (Keeble 2012).

Stephen Dorril, in his history of MI6, reports that in 1944 Astor was transferred to a unit liaising between SOE and the Resistance in France, helping the French underground in London spread the word to groups throughout Europe (Dorril 2000: 457). While in Paris, perhaps inspired by Astor, Orwell attended the first conference of the Committee for European Federation, bringing together

Resistance groups from around Europe. The French novelist and editor of *Combat*, Albert Camus, was amongst those present – though they failed to meet. Astor was later adamant that Orwell had no intelligence links[3] and Peter Davison, editor of Orwell's twenty-volume collected works, commented: 'I doubt if Orwell would be involved with intelligence – but that by no means says he wasn't.'[4]

All this suggests that Orwell's controversial decision to submit a 'little list' of 38 'crypto-communists' (briefly and somewhat crudely) to his friend, the sister-in-law of the author Arthur Koestler, Celia Kirwan (née Paget) when she was working as Robert Conquest's assistant for the secret state's newly-formed propaganda unit, the Information Research Department, was not an aberration (as generally thought).[5] Rather, it was an action consistent with his attitudes and behaviour as they developed during the 1940s – particularly through his friendship with David Astor.[6]

Moreover, during Orwell's final years, Astor played an enormously important role. It was he who persuaded Aneurin Bevan, Orwell's old *Tribune* editor, by now Secretary of State for Health in the Attlee government, to allow the special importation of the very expensive drug, streptomycin, from the United States to treat his friend's TB (Taylor 2003: 392).[7] It was he who owned the land on the remote Scottish island of Jura where Orwell spent his final days bashing out the *Nineteen Eighty-Four* manuscript. Astor also paid for the private room (No. 65) at University College Hospital where Orwell was to marry Sonia Brownell (with Astor as Best Man) and spend his last days. It was he who hosted the lunch at the Ritz following the wedding (Orwell was too ill to attend). And after Orwell, the atheist and unpredictable to the very end, asked in his will to be buried in a churchyard, Astor found a plot at All Saints, Sutton Courtenay, Oxfordshire, close to his family estate.[8]

There were clearly many influences on Orwell in the making of *Nineteen Eighty-Four*. Yet, given Orwell's introduction to the world of spooks by his friend Astor, is it not surprising then that his last great novel should describe a world of Big Brother, of child spies and telescreens – and where the state's surveillance intrudes into the individual's innermost private life? Orwell's ambivalent attitude to just about everything was reflected in his responses to the secret state. On the one hand, he supported it and became friends with some of its operators. But he also saw the secret state's growing powers and was horrified. So he dedicated all his energy (in what proved to be his final years) in his remote house on Jura to composing the crucial warning. And his representation of Julia in *Nineteen Eighty-Four* was also profoundly influenced by his concerns over the political and epistemological implications of the growth of the secret state.

RICHARD LANCE KEEBLE

JULIA: IS SHE BASED ON SONIA?

An intriguing number of elements in *Nineteen Eighty-Four* have close personal ties to Orwell. For instance, Winston begins writing his diary on 4 April – the day after the funeral of his first wife, Eileen O'Shaughnessy (in 1945);[9] Eileen had also, significantly, written a poem 'End of the Century, 1984' marking the 50th anniversary of her school in 1934 and looking ahead to the next half century (Bowker 2003: 382); Winston is said to be 39 – precisely the age his son, Richard, would be in 1984; the place where Winston is tortured by O'Brien at the end of the novel is given the number 101, satirically, after the room at the BBC where Orwell attended many boring meetings during his time working there between 1941 and 1943 – and so on. Inevitably, then, a number of writers have suggested that Julia is closely based on Sonia Brownell. For instance, Hilary Spurling, in her sympathetic, short biography of Sonia, writes (2002: 93):

> Memories of Sonia – her youth and prettiness, her toughness, above all her radiant vitality – fed directly into the book's heroine (who puts in a sixty-hour week or more tending to the literary machines in the offices of the Fiction Department at the Ministry of Truth). Sonia's imagined presence kept company with Orwell on the island of Jura as Julia's comforted his hero, Winston.

But according to Dorian Lynskey (2019: 174), there is little to link Sonia and Julia: 'Orwell was also close to Inez Holden and Celia Paget and he saw more of them while writing *Nineteen Eighty-Four* than he did of Sonia. Sonia and the dark-haired Julia didn't look alike, and they certainly didn't think alike.'

D. J. Taylor suggests the evidence for the Julia/Sonia identification is mixed. On the one hand: 'Orwell, at the time he first asked Sonia to marry him, was in his early forties. In both cases, a distinctly unhealthy middle-aged man is obsessed with an energetic woman in her twenties' (2019: 40). Like Sonia, Julia has a forceful presence but while Winston notes of Julia that 'Except for her mouth, you could not have called her beautiful' Sonia was well known for her striking good looks (ibid). Moreover, Orwell had begun the novel well before he became involved with Sonia.

Taylor suggests that traces of a number of other women are to be found in Julia. The sexual encounters with Julia *en plein air* recall his relationship with Eleanor Jaques in Suffolk in the early 1930s while Julia's 'swift, athletic movements' recall Brenda Salkend, a gym mistress and another of Orwell's loves in Suffolk in the early 1930s (ibid: 41). Julia's significance in the book, Taylor argues, is 'figurative rather than decisive': symbolising youth, impulse, free-spiritedness. Certainly, towards the end of the novel, when Winston is being tortured with the rats cage in Room 101, Julia becomes the focus of his symbolically ultimate betrayal: 'Do it to Julia! Do it to Julia! Not me! Julia! I don't care what you do to her. Tear her face off, strip her to the bones. Not me! Julia! Not me!' he cries (Orwell 2000 [1949]: 329).

THE FEMINIST CRITIQUE

Orwell's representation of Julia has drawn particular wrath from feminist critics. For Daphne Patai, Orwell evokes yet another female stereotype: she is motivated only by a love of sexual pleasure and is totally uninterested in the political dynamics of the society that oppresses her (Patai 1984: 243). When Winston reads to her from the book, supposedly written by the leader of the rebellion, Goldstein, she falls asleep (ibid: 244). Patai also suggests Orwell's naming of the central characters reflects his sexist bias (ibid: 244):

> Julia has only a first name; she is an insignificant female, and Orwell in this respect follows his society's convention of considering a woman's last name a disposable, because changeable, element in an uncertain social identity. O'Brien, at the opposite pole, has only a last name, in typical masculine style. And Winston Smith, halfway between powerless personal feminine and the powerful impersonal masculine, has a complete name, albeit an ironic one in that it combines the legendary with the commonplace.

According to Beatrix Campbell (1984: 129), women simply 'do not appear as protagonists in Orwell's working class'. On *Nineteen Eighty-Four*, she comments: 'Julia is Winston's sleeping partner in sedition. Her rebellion is essentially sexual. She's promiscuous, she's had hundreds of men and her subversion is sealed in an equation between corruption and sexuality.' This reduction of Julia to her corrupt biology renders her rebellion 'as something seething below the threshold of political consciousness' (ibid). Similarly, Deidre Beddoe, in her essay 'Women in the writings of George Orwell', acknowledges that Julia shows courage, flouts the minor and then the major rules of the totalitarian society – and initiates contact with Winston. But she adds (1984: 147):

> The protests of Winston and Julia are inspired by totally different motives. Whereas Winston is inspired by intellectual concepts like the integrity of history and the notion of freedom, Julia is only 'a rebel from the waist downwards'. The sexually attractive and sexually active Julia objects to the regime because it stops here having a good time.

For Christopher Hitchens, hardly noted as a feminist (2002: 105): 'Every one of the female characters [in his novels] is practically devoid of the least trace of intellectual or reflective capacity.'

RICHARD LANCE KEEBLE

MALE IDEALISATIONS OF JULIA

Contrasting with the damning feminist critique of the Julia representation, the (mostly male) biographers have tended to idealise her. Michael Shelden, for instance, comments (1991: 472): 'For Julia and Winston, sex becomes a form of liberation, a way not only of rebelling against the dictates of the Party, but also a means by which they can enjoy a sense of freedom in the release of passion... It is an affirmation of life in the face of Big Brother's attempt to eliminate all signs of vital existence among his subjects.' Robert Colls is almost ecstatic in his adulation (2013: 215-216):

> She is a 26-year-old mechanic – a technical woman, once of the new middle class that Orwell had reached out to in the late 1930s – smart, young, self-aware, unsnobbish and competent in all the ways Winston is not. She does as she pleases. She is practical. She is instinctual. She is effective. She gives him hope. She shows him how. She tells him where. ... The most important words in the book have nothing to do with the proles or Big Brother or Room 101: 'We are dead,' he said. 'We're not dead yet,' said Julia prosaically.

According to Jeffrey Meyers (2000: 284):

> Like Winston she is a symbolic figure. When she brings chocolate to their first meeting the smell of it stirs a troubling memory in Winston. Later, in bed with Julia, he wakes and remembers the day he stole the family's chocolate ration was the same day that his mother and sister disappeared. The chocolate connects Julia with his lost mother's love and helps relieve his guilt for his mother's death. Julia represents the power of instinctive feeling and the continuity of love.

James Preece (2019) even argues that Julia is 'the clearest indication of feminism (in substance, if not in word) in Orwell's late writing', adding: 'Julia's sense of politics comes from freedom – freedom to love, to have sex and to be herself in the countryside.' While for Dorian Lynskey, Julia represents a third way to live under Ingsoc (2019: 174):

> O'Brien claims there is no such thing as objective truth; Winston insists there is; Julia maintains that *it doesn't matter* (italics in the original). Because she can't remember the past and doesn't care about the future, she lives entirely in the present, which is what the Party wants. ... In some ways, she is cleverer than Winston, intuiting that Goldstein and the revolutionary Brotherhood are probably fictions concocted by the Party, but it is a cynical, even nihilistic intelligence.

NINETEEN EIGHTY-FOUR'S SEXUAL POLITICS

Sexual politics lie at the heart of *Nineteen Eighty-Four*. According to Cass R. Sunstein (2005: 241):

> Orwell suggests that totalitarian governments favour 'sexual puritanism', which induces 'hysteria', something that such governments mobilize in their own favour. This is the image of patriotic frenzy as 'sex gone sour'. On this view, sexual freedom embodies freedom and individualism, and it is the deepest enemy of a totalitarian state. A state that allows sexual freedom will be unable to repress its citizens.

Orwell represents Oceana as hyper-puritanical: the aim of Party is to remove all pleasure from the sexual act; all marriages have to be approved by committee; permission is refused if the couple give the impression of being physically attracted to one another; the only recognised purpose of marriage is to beget children to serve the Party; sexual intercourse is seen as a slightly disgusting minor operation, like having an enema – and the Junior Anti-Sex league advocates complete celibacy for both sexes (Orwell 2000 [1949]: 75). In addition, all children are to be begotten by artificial insemination (artsem in Newspeak) and raised in public institutions. At the same time, promiscuity is permitted amongst the proles – and pornography is produced specially for them in Pornosec, a sub-section of the Fiction Department (ibid: 50). Towards the end of the novel, as O'Brien tortures Winston, he pronounces (ibid: 306):

> We have cut the links between child and parent, and between man and man, and between man and woman. No one dares trust a wife or a child or a friend any longer. But in the future there will be no wives and no friends. … The sex instinct will be eradicated. Procreation will be an annual formality like the renewal of a ration card. We shall abolish the orgasm.

In this context, the passionate affair Winston has with Julia acquires added symbolic significance. As Robin West stresses (2005: 248): 'Erotic sex, Winston Smith insists in *Nineteen Eighty-Four*, is a truly *political* and even revolutionary act.' In contrast to the sexually promiscuous Julia, Winston's wife, Katharine, is represented (quite mercilessly) as a frigid bore:

> As soon as he touched her she seemed to wince and stiffen. To embrace her was like embracing a jointed wooden image. … They must, she said, produce a child if they could. So the performance continued to happen, once a week quite regularly, whenever it was not impossible. … But luckily no child appeared and in the end she agreed to give up trying, and soon afterwards they parted (Orwell 2000 [1949]: 76).

Daphne Patai is particularly critical of Orwell's depiction of sexuality in the novel. Though Julia is said to have had many affairs, nowhere are the problems associated with contraception and abortion considered (1984: 247). The only reference to the biological facts of reproduction appear when Julia cancels a meeting with Winston because 'it's started early this time' (Orwell 2000 [1949]: 160). 'This delicate reference to menstruation, and the assumption that it prevents intercourse (apparently the sole object of Julia and Winston's meetings) is reiterated when Winston reflects that this "particular disappointment must be a normal, recurring event" in marriage' (ibid: 161).

IS JULIA A SPY?

But what if Julia is actually a member of the Party, luring Winston Smith into a honeytrap? Orwell certainly offers various hints that he wants us to at least ponder this question. When Winston first sees Julia at the Two Minute Hate session, she arrives with O'Brien – who first befriends and then turns into his torturer in Room 101 (ibid: 12). Why? Are they friends? Is it just a coincidence? Even Winston wonders: 'The idea had even crossed his mind that she might be an agent of the Thought Police. That, it was true, was very unlikely. Still, he continued to feel a peculiar uneasiness, which had fear mixed up in it as well as hostility, whenever she was anywhere near him' (ibid: 13). He next sees her in the canteen: 'His earlier thought returned to him: probably she was not actually a member of the Thought Police, but then it was precisely the amateur spy who was the greatest danger of all' (ibid: 71).

Perhaps the strongest hint Orwell offers that Julia is actually a spy occurs when Winston, on the spur of the moment, decides to take a walk through London's backstreets. But then, whom does he see walking towards him: none other than the 'girl from the Fiction Department' (ibid: 115). 'She looked him straight in the face, then walked quickly on as though she had not seen him.' And Winston ponders:

> There was no doubting any longer that the girl was spying on him. She must have followed him here, because it was not credible that by pure chance she should have happened to be walking on the same evening up the same obscure backstreet, kilometres distant from any quarter where Party members lived. Whether she was an agent of the Thought Police, or simply an amateur spy actuated by officiousness, hardly mattered. It was enough that she was watching him (ibid).

When Julia and Winston meet for sex for the first time, there is this extraordinary conversation (ibid: 139):

> 'What is your name?' said Winston. 'Julia. I know yours. It's Winston – Winston Smith.' 'How did you find that out?' 'I expect I'm better at finding things out than you are, dear.'

In other words, is not Julia revealing all the attributes of a conscientious spy – knowing the name of her target, for instance? And as if to confirm the reader's suspicions, Orwell adds: 'He began telling her the story of his married life but curiously enough she appeared to know the essential parts of it already' (as, indeed, would not a well-briefed spy?).

Winston is later arrested along with Julia by the Thought Police in their love nest above Charrington's junk shop. But is Julia actually tortured – like Winston – in the Ministry of Love? We never really know. At the end, they meet by chance in a park. Each admits betraying the other under torture. But we can never be sure on anything about Julia.

SO WHAT?

Seeing Julia as a spy can lead to two contrasting interpretations. On the one hand it can be seen as subverting the conventional image of her: instead of being a submissive sex object she becomes a highly politicised agent of the state, influencing events in major ways. And her falling asleep just as Winston begins to read from Emmanuel Goldstein's dissident political tract, *The Theory and Practice of Oligarchic Collectivism*, can now appear in a completely different light: it's not because she's unpolitical and unintelligent as Orwell's feminist critics have argued (see Patai 1984: 244) but, as a spy, she is completely uninterested in it.

On the other hand, as Tim Crook (2018) argues: 'There is still a valid feminist criticism of this dimension of the characterisation in deploying and demeaning the woman as a stereotypical Mata Hari-type honeytrap where women feature almost exclusively as the corrupting and seducing agents of sexpionage.'

THE JULIA CONUNDRUM AND EPISTEMOLOGY

The Julia Conundrum is best understood within the broader context of Orwell's reflections on truth and objectivity in both his writings in general – and in *Nineteen Eighty-Four*, in particular. Perhaps with a touch of irony and dark humour, Orwell has Winston engaging in an esoteric, philosophical discussion with O'Brien in the torture room at the Ministry of Love about a wide range of topics: the nature of meaning, truth, metaphysics, solipsism, power, freedom, death and the transience of life, reality, human identity, sexuality, family life, history, the individual's autonomy (or lack of it) and the nature of existence. Added to this brew are some rather strange/spooky readings of Winston's mind by O'Brien. For instance, on the question of objective truth, O'Brien comments (Orwell 2000 [1949]: 285):

> You believe that reality is something objective, external, existing in its own right. You also believe that the nature of reality is self-evident. ... But I tell you, Winston, that reality is not external.

RICHARD LANCE KEEBLE

Reality exists in the human mind and nowhere else. Not in the individual mind, which can make mistakes, and in any case soon perishes: only in the mind of the Party which is collective and immortal. Whatever the Party holds to be truth, *is* truth. It is impossible to see reality except by looking through the eyes of the Party.

Winston ponders: the belief that nothing exists outside your own mind – surely there must be some way of demonstrating it was false? (ibid: 305). But immediately, O'Brien, displaying remarkable 'mind-reading' abilities chips in: 'I told you, Winston … that metaphysics is not your strong point. The word you are trying to think of is solipsism. But you are mistaken. This is not solipsism. Collective solipsism, if you like.' And to illustrate Oceana's contempt for objective truth, O'Brien holds up four fingers and demands that Winston, under torture, admit there are five (ibid: 286).

As David Dwan comments (2019: 153): 'Winston is a convinced empiricist – a firm believer in the "evidence of your senses", or the "evidence of your eyes and ears" as the foundation for knowledge.' And much of the rhetoric in Orwell's writings asserts the importance of democracy's belief in objective truth. Totalitarian regimes not only circulated lies, they attacked the very 'concept of objective truth' (ibid: 144).

In contrast, O'Brien's rejection of mind-independent reality leads him to cast aside (somewhat ludicrously) all external restrictions on the will. 'He makes no concessions to the friction of the world: "I could float off this floor like a soap bubble if I wished to." So O'Brien cannot even tolerate gravitational laws and claims a kind of freedom that many Christians had denied even to God' (ibid: 158).

Yet, as Dwan stresses, while Winston supports the idea of truth, it is significantly never made clear in the novel what truth really is (ibid: 152). Indeed, as on so many issues, Orwell's reflections throughout his writings on epistemological issues were ambivalent, contradictory – or both. He certainly had little difficulty in telling lies for political ends. While working for the Eastern Overseas Services of the BBC in 1942, he confided to his diary for 3 March:

> Our radio strategy is even more hopeless than our military strategy. Nevertheless one rapidly becomes propaganda-minded and develops a cunning one did not previously have. Eg. I am regularly alleging in my newsletters that the Japanese are plotting to attack Russia. I don't believe this to be so (Orwell 2009: 224).

In *Homage to Catalonia* (1962 [1938]), his account of his time fighting alongside Republican militia men during the Spanish civil war, he outlines his ambivalence in a different way: 'I have tried to write objectively about the Barcelona fighting, though, obviously, no one can be completely objective on a question of this kind. One is practically obliged to take sides and it must be clear enough which side I am on' (ibid: 153).

Within this broad epistemological context, then, the Julia Conundrum serves to highlight the essential unknowingness of reality. Is Julia a spy? Orwell typically teases the reader with a number of clues. Indeed, Orwell loved to give the readers of his 'As I Please' column in the leftist journal *Tribune* (from 1943-1947) brain teases – which he dubbed 'brain ticklers' (see Keeble 2007). For instance, on 7 July 1944, he concluded his column with this 'intelligence test' (see Anderson 2006: 160): 'A man walked four miles due south from his house and shot a bear. He then walked two miles due west, then walked another four miles due north and was back at his home again. What was the colour of the bear?' (The answer, given in his 28 July column, is white: the man lived at the North Pole and the bear must, therefore, be a polar bear.) In the world of *Nineteen Eighty-Four*, O'Brien gives Winston a brain teaser: does the dissident Brotherhood exist? And he tells his victim: 'As long as you live it will be an unsolved riddle in your mind.' Similarly, for readers of the novel whether Julia is actually a spy or not will remain forever an 'unsolved riddle'.

CONCLUSIONS

This paper has sought to locate the representation of Julia in *Nineteen Eighty-Four* within the context of Orwell's personal involvement in the secret state – as well as his reflections (and warnings) on the political, social and cultural elements of his imagined hyper-dictatorial Big Brother state and its radical epistemological implications. For in a society dominated by secret intelligence (with all its brutality, Thought Police, torture, constant surveillance, child spies and propaganda) any notion of 'objective truth' is eliminated. Intelligence, after all, can never be double-checked: by definition its source remains secret and exclusive. It could all be fiction – and often is. As a former foreign secretary, Lord Howe, told the Scott arms-to-Iraq inquiry in 1992: 'In my early days I was naïve enough to get excited about intelligence reports. Many look, at first sight, to be important and interesting and significant and then when we check them they are not even straws in the wind. They are cornflakes in the wind' (Norton-Taylor 2003).

Moreover, seeing Julia as a possible spy makes the novel even darker since her secret affair with Winston is one of its very few bright features – allowing Winston at least a few moments of escape from Oceana's grim reality.

Gordon Bowker, in his biography of Orwell (2003: 388) argues that, more than any other novel, *Nineteen Eighty-Four* is concerned with role-playing and deception: the Party is deceiving everyone, Julia is deceiving the Anti-Sex League, Charrington, the junk shop owner and O'Brien are deceiving Winston, Winston is deceiving himself. He continues, significantly raising questions about Julia's identity:

> 'Truth' is also a deception because the Party controls the present, past and future. Once this 'shifting reality' is established, no one can be taken at face value. Julia seems to be a secret hater of the Party and Big Brother, seems to be a candidate for the dissident Brotherhood, seems to go off to be tortured after her arrest and finally seems to have been purged of her thoughtcrime. But in the world of the book she could, like O'Brien and Charrington, also be a dissembler leading Winston straight into the arms of the Thought Police. On Airstrip One truth rests on ever-shifting sands, only pain and Room 101 are real.

The Julia Conundrum can also be linked with Orwell's broader literary project. One of the most perceptive analyses of Orwell's *oeuvre* is provided by Lynette Hunter (1984). She argues that his ambivalences, contradictions and inconsistencies emerge from his essential approach to writing and learning:

> The assumption that one can absolutely define Orwell in biographical terms is parallel to the assumption that his writing and message or interpretation are equally clear and fixed. But the very attempt to define and fix into stasis is part of a world view that Orwell rejected. If this is not recognized then the outcome is often the suggestion that Orwell is being inconsistent, hence untrustworthy and deceitful (ibid: 10).

For Hunter, Orwell's approach is always questioning and educational as he invites his readers to join him in his quest for learning.

> All too often there is an unwillingness to accept that Orwell might learn, come to appreciate different things and change his mind, and to recognize that this apparent inconsistency overlays a fundamentally consistent belief in the need to evaluate actively, never to assume the quality of axioms and fixed standards (ibid).

Orwell's literary voice, above all, Hunter argues 'does not impose opinion on others but invites discussion' (ibid: 11).

Similarly, David Dwan says Orwell's overall *oeuvre* 'raises troubling questions about his own inconsistencies and doubletalk' (2019: 206). He adds: 'Contrary to what many have assumed, Orwell provides few solutions to our political difficulties, although this was never his job. As Hilary Putnam once suggested, the writer's task is not to deliver solutions but to engage in the "imaginative re-creation of moral perplexities".'

Indeed, highlighting the Julia Conundrum (and the question readers are invited to consider: is Julia a spy?) ties in not only with Orwell's epistemological uncertainties and concerns about the growing powers of the secret state – but it also gives the book a strangely modern character, making it a novel about the slippery, unstable nature of meaning.

NOTES

[1] Knightley, Phillip (1986: 131). In 1956, Astor was persuaded to offer cover for the SIS agent (later to be revealed as a Soviet spy), Kim Philby, as a journalist in Beirut

[2] *Tribune* was later to be distributed to British missions abroad by the Information Research Department

[3] In an interview with the author, London, November 1999

[4] In a letter to the author, 7 December 1999

[5] 'Known' suspects include Labour MPs, the future Poet Laureate Cecil Day-Lewis, authors J. B. Priestley and John Steinbeck, journalist Richard Crossman, actors Michael Redgrave, Charlie Chaplin and Paul Robeson, actor and director Orson Welles, and the historians A. J. P. Taylor and Isaac Deutscher

[6] It is ironic, then, that Orwell was followed closely by British intelligence from the time of his first publication in *Monde*, edited by the communist Henri Barbusse, in Paris, in 1929 until his death (see Keeble 2012). Orwell's great friend, an Old-Etonian, the novelist Anthony Powell, had also worked for intelligence during the war

[7] Taylor op cit: 392. The treatment unfortunately did not work

[8] Crick op cit: 580

[9] See https://www.irishtimes.com/opinion/stop-all-the-clocks-frank-mcnally-on-the-influence-of-george-orwell-s-first-wife-eileen-o-shaughnessy-on-1984-1.3923580, accessed on 22 June 2019

REFERENCES

Anderson, Paul (ed.) (2006) *Orwell in* Tribune, London: Politico's

Beddoe, Deirdre (1984) Hindrances and help-meets: Women in the writings of George Orwell, Norris, Christopher (ed.) *Inside the Myth: Orwell: Views from the Left*, London: Lawrence and Wishart pp 139-154

Bowker, Gordon (2003) *George Orwell*, London: Little, Brown

Cabell, Craig (2008) *Ian Fleming's Secret War*, Barnsley, South Yorkshire: Pen and Sword

Campbell, Beatrix (1984) Orwell: Paterfamilias or Big Brother?, Norris, Christopher (ed.) *Inside the Myth: Orwell: Views from the Left*, London: Lawrence and Wishart pp 128-136

Colls, Robert (2013) *George Orwell: English Rebel*, Oxford: Oxford University Press

Crick, Bernard (1980) *George Orwell: A Life*, Harmondsworth, Middlesex: Penguin

Crook, Tim (2018) On Julia and sexpionage, in an email to the author, 20 September 2018

Dorril, Stephen (2000) *MI6: Fifty Years of Special Operations*, London: Fourth Estate

Dwan, David (2019) *Liberty, Equality and Humbug: Orwell's Political Ideals*, Oxford: Oxford University Press

Hitchens, Christopher (2001) *Orwell's Victory*, London: Penguin

Hunter, Lynette (1984) *George Orwell: The Search for a Voice*, Milton Keynes: Open University Press

Keeble, Richard (2007) The lasting in the ephemeral: Assessing George Orwell's 'As I Please' columns, Keeble, Richard and Wheeler, Sharon (eds) *The Journalistic Imagination: Literary Journalists From Defoe to Capote and Carter*, Routledge: London pp 100-115

Keeble, Richard Lance (2012) Orwell, *Nineteen Eighty-Four* and the spooks, Keeble, Richard Lance (ed.) *Orwell Today*, Bury St Edmunds: Abramis pp 151-163

Knightley, Phillip (1986) *The Second Oldest Profession: The Spy as Bureaucrat, Patriot, Fantasist and Whore*, London: André Deutsch

Lewis, Jeremy (2016) *David Astor*, London: Jonathan Cape

Lynskey, Dorian (2019) *The Ministry of Truth: A Biography of George Orwell's 1984*, London: Picador

Macintyre, Ben (2014) *A Spy Among Friends: Philby and the Great Betrayal*, London: Bloomsbury

Meyers, Jeffrey (2000) *Orwell: Wintry Conscience of a Generation*, New York and London: W. W. Norton and Company Ltd

Norton-Taylor, Richard (2003) The BBC now has been got up to obscure the ugly truth, *Guardian*, 28 June

Orwell, George (1962 [1938]) *Homage to Catalonia*, Harmondsworth, Middlesex: Penguin

Orwell, George (2000 [1949]) *Nineteen Eighty-Four*, London: Penguin Classics

Orwell George (2009) *Diaries*, Davison, Peter (ed.) London: Penguin

Patai, Daphne (1984) *The Orwell Mystique: A Study in Male Ideology*, Amherst: University of Massachusetts Press

Porter, Bernard (1989) *Plots and Paranoia: A History of Political Espionage in Britain 1790-1988*, London: Unwin Hyman

Preece, James (2019) The secrets of *Nineteen Eighty-Four*, *International Socialism*, Issue 163. Available online at http://isj.org.uk/the-secrets-of-nineteen-eighty-four/, accessed on 9 August 2019

Shelden, Michael (1991) *Orwell: The Authorised Biography*, London: William Heinemann

Spurling, Hilary (2003) *The Girl from the Fiction Department: A Portrait of Sonia Brownell*, London: Penguin

Taylor, D. J. (2003) *Orwell: The Life*, London: Chatto and Windus

Taylor, D. J. (2019) Who was Julia? *Nineteen Eighty-Four*'s many heroines, *George Orwell Studies*, Vol. 3, No. 2 pp 39-43

ARTICLES

Memoirs of Orwell:
The Quest for the Truth

The memoirs of Orwell are valuable sources for his biographers who are always keen to find new material and vivid details, says Jeffrey Meyers. The authors describe personal details, narrate significant events in his life, reveal his strange personality and portray the culture in which he lived. Here Meyers places the memoirs in the context of the authors' lives and their relations with Orwell.

George Orwell (1903-1950) inspired seventeen important memoirs, published between 1938 and 1982, by friends and acquaintances who were eager to write about him. Their viewpoints range from reverence and awe to condescension and hostility. They were intrigued by Orwell's unusual appearance and impressively eccentric character and emphasised his personal idiosyncrasies rather than his artistic achievement. The memoirs of Orwell are valuable sources for his biographers who are always keen to find new material and vivid details. His life-writers must extract the gold and reject the dross, clear the minefield of errors and establish the truth, and shape these different accounts into a coherent and convincing portrait.

These various, sometimes conflicting characterisations of Orwell portray his life in miniature. He appears as a prep school boy, Etonian, Burmese policeman, investigator of down-and-outs and coal miners, volunteer soldier in Spain, journalist and essayist, wartime propagandist at the BBC, highly praised author of two political satires as well as difficult husband, devoted father and doomed tubercular on the remote Scottish island of Jura. The authors describe personal details, narrate significant events in his life, reveal his strange personality and portray the culture in which he lived. This article places the memoirs in the context of the authors' lives and their relations with Orwell.

Orwell's lifelong friendship with the porcine and witty Cyril Connolly began at their prep school St. Cyprian's and at Eton, and lasted through Orwell's contributions to *Horizon* and deathbed marriage to Connolly's secretary, Sonia Brownell, who queened it up as his wealthy widow. In *Enemies of Promise* (1960 [1938]), the only memoir published during Orwell's lifetime, Connolly portrays their prep school as merely Spartan and snobbish, rather than as the cruel and terrifying prison that Orwell describes in 'Such, Such Were the Joys'. Connolly writes: 'I was a stage rebel, Orwell a true one. Tall, pale, with his flaccid cheeks, large spatulate fingers, and supercilious voice, he was one of those boys who seem born old' (p. 170). He remembers Orwell's independence: 'He thought for himself … rejected not only [St. Cyprian's], but the [1914] war, the Empire, Kipling, Sussex, and Character.' Orwell gloomily but accurately predicted 'whoever wins this war, we shall emerge as a second-rate nation'. At Eton, the intellectual and aloof Orwell was nicknamed 'Cynicus' and was 'perpetually sneering at "They" – a Marxist-Shavian concept which included Masters, Old Collegers, the Church and Senior reactionaries' (p. 194).

In later books, Connolly notes that during World War II Orwell 'felt enormously at home in the Blitz, among the bombs, the bravery, the rubble, the shortages, the homeless, the signs of rising revolutionary temper' (quoted in Meyers 2000: 196). Connolly concludes by summing up the tragedy of Orwell's life: 'When at last he achieved fame and success [with *Animal Farm* and *Nineteen Eighty-Four*] he was a dying man and knew it. He had fame and was too ill to leave his [hospital] room, money and nothing to spend it on, love in which he could not participate; he tasted the bitterness of dying' (Meyers: 313).

Orwell defined the moral chasm between himself and his old friend when he caustically wrote of Connolly's first novel *The Rock Pool* (1947): 'Even to want to write about so-called artists who spend on sodomy what they have gained by sponging betrays a kind of spiritual inadequacy' (Meyers: 169). He felt that the portly Connolly had been fatally weakened by sloth, self-pity and an inordinate taste for luxury. Connolly's memories were influenced by his realisation that Orwell's idealism and spectacular achievements provided a striking contrast to his own hedonism and failure to fulfil his potential.

Connolly, Orwell's rival, had reservations about his old friend. By contrast, the obituary in the *Observer* of 29 January 1950 (reprinted in *The Trail of the Dinosaur*, 1955) by the fiercely combative Arthur Koestler is filled with admiration and esteem. After the sudden death of his wife, Eileen, in 1945, Orwell impulsively proposed to Celia Paget, the stunning twin sister of Koestler's wife. Koestler enthusiastically supported this idea and wanted Orwell to strengthen their bond and become his brother-in-law, but he could not persuade Celia to marry a man she didn't love.

Koestler's tribute emphasises his friend's uncompromising and almost inhuman intellectual honesty: '[He was] severe upon his friends, unresponsive to admirers, but full of understanding sympathy for those on the remote periphery. ... His ruthlessness towards himself was the key to his personality; it determined his attitude towards the enemy within, the disease which had raged in his chest since his adolescence' (pp 102-103). Koestler considers Orwell the missing link between Swift and Kafka, the only genius among the writers of social revolt between the wars: 'No parable written since *Gulliver's Travels* was equal in profundity and mordant satire to *Animal Farm*, no fantasy since Kafka's *In the Penal Settlement* equal in logical horror to *1984*' (p. 104).

Christopher Hollis, Orwell's contemporary at Eton, went to Oxford and became a publisher, Catholic convert and Tory MP. Like Connolly, his early *Study of George Orwell* (1956) states that Orwell exaggerated his sufferings at prep school and argues that he was a natural solitary who suffered from a sense of sin and guilt. Hollis records some of the young Orwell's learned and provocative assertions: 'I'm collecting the religions of the new boys. Are you Cyreniac, Sceptic, Epicurean, Cynic, Neoplatonist, Confucian or Zoroastrian?' 'I'm a Christian.' 'Oh, we haven't had that before' (p. 15). When a master made a weak threat by declaring: 'Things can't go on like this. Either you or I will have to go,' Orwell cheekily replied: 'I'm afraid it'll have to be you, sir' (p. 17).

The balding, stuttering, desperately poor and dissolute Paul Potts printed and sold his own poems in Soho pubs – until he was banned for bad behaviour. In 'Don Quixote on a bicycle: In memoriam, George Orwell' (1957), Orwell's disciple emphasises his kindness, independence, courage, integrity, Englishness, conversation, hobbies and capacity for hard work during his short writing life of only seventeen years. He describes Orwell's reaction to the death of Eileen when he was reporting the war in Germany for the *Observer* in 1945 and (like Koestler) his devotion to their adopted infant Richard.

Though Orwell was notorious for his deplorable taste in food – he once ate eels left out for the cat – the half-starved Potts offers an idealised picture, right out of Dickens, of a bountiful meal at Orwell's flat in Canonbury Square, London: 'A huge fire, the table crowded with marvellous things, gentleman's relish and various jams, kippers, crumpets and toast' (p. 40). Potts's essay does not mention Orwell's meeting with Ernest Hemingway in liberated Paris in the spring of 1945. But when he reprinted it and wanted to flesh out his thin book *Dante Called You Beatrice* (1960), he invented a stereotyped encounter between the shy Englishman and the blustering American, a meeting that Hemingway accurately portrayed in his posthumous memoir *True at First Light* (1999).

ARTICLE

JEFFREY MEYERS

'My brother, George Orwell' (1961) – by his rather sour younger sister Avril Blair Dunn – was recorded for the BBC in 1960. She says their elderly father was the youngest of twelve children, describes Orwell's pleasant childhood in Henley-on-Thames and a family where emotions were suppressed. She writes, with some irritation, of how Burma had affected Orwell's character when he returned to England in 1927: 'Being used to a lot of servants he'd become terribly – to our minds – untidy. Whenever he smoked a cigarette he threw the end down on the floor – and the match – and expected other people [like herself] to sweep them up' (p. 257). She portrays their harsh life together in the primitive farmhouse on Jura, and convincingly maintains that his tuberculosis could have been cured after his first stay in a sanatorium if he had not insisted on returning to the bleak Hebridean island to write *Nineteen Eighty-Four*.

After Eileen's death, Avril took care of their child; she married the farmer Bill Dunn in 1951 and brought up Richard in Scotland. (Critics often mention that when Richard was born Orwell put him down for Westminster, but that did not reflect his real attitude towards elite schools. In the end, Richard went to Loretto private school, near Edinburgh, and then on to an agricultural college before becoming a representative of Massey Ferguson, the farm equipment firm.)

Rayner Heppenstall was born in Yorkshire, graduated from Leeds University and became a minor poet, novelist and balletomane. In 1935, he shared a Kentish Town flat with Orwell and Michael Sayers, and in *Four Absentees* (1960) recalled that Orwell did most of the cooking and housekeeping, and had a succession of dreary girlfriends. He condescendingly wrote that 'both Michael and I regarded Eric [his real name] as a nice old thing, a kindly eccentric. We liked him, but we did not always take him seriously. For my own part, I even tended to exploit him a little' (p. 59). With some exaggeration, he declared that Orwell hated Scots, 'bishops, civil servants, RC's, well-to-do Bohemians, psychiatrists, Wyndham Lewis' and Middleton Murry (p. 62). When Heppenstall came home drunk in the middle of the night, woke Orwell up and took a swing at him, Orwell punched him in the face and knocked him down. Ten minutes later Heppenstall came to, lying on the floor and covered in blood, and saw in Orwell's face a 'curious blend of fear and sadistic exaltation' (p. 86).

In a rare confessional moment, Orwell told Heppenstall that he thought he was biologically sterile. Heppenstall visited Wallington, a desolate village in Berkshire, where Orwell kept a failing store and farm, with two goats in a stinking shed next to a decrepit cottage. But he was pleased to see that Orwell and the attractive Eileen, after their marriage in 1936, 'behaved with conspicuous affection' (p. 146). Heppenstall portrays a prejudiced oddball, 'a curious mind, satirically attached to everything traditionally English … but arid, colourless, devoid of poetry, derisive, yet darkly obsessed' (p. 63). He later wrote that Orwell had adopted a fake persona and deliberately cultivated a proletarian style and eccentric manner that helped promote the Orwell legend. In the 1960s, Heppenstall complained of 'a whole Orwell mythology which seemed to bear little relation to the man I had known' (Meyers: 92). Disappointed in his own career and envious of Orwell's success with *Animal Farm*, Heppenstall published the most patronising and caustic portrait of Orwell.

Sir Richard Rees was educated at Eton and Trinity College, Cambridge, served in the diplomatic service, worked for Cambridge University Press and taught at the Workers' Educational Association. Thin, bald and deep-voiced, he drove an ambulance during the Spanish civil war and won the Croix de Guerre in World War II. He published Orwell's early work in the *Adelphi*, while Orwell portrayed his close friend and patron as Ravelston, the socialist editor of a 'middle to high-brow monthly' in his novel *Keep the Aspidistra Flying* (1936). He wrote that the character based on Rees was 'a tall distinguished figure, aristocratically shabby, his eye rather moody. … Ravelston had not merely a charm of manner, but also a kind of fundamental decency, a graceful attitude to life' (Meyers: 94).

In *George Orwell: Fugitive from the Camp of Victory* (1962), Rees makes some perceptive observations. Though Orwell and Eileen were both ill, 'they underfed themselves during the war, in order to share their rations with people whose need they judged greater than their own' (p. 140). After visiting Jura, he calls Orwell's primitive dwelling 'the most uninhabitable house in the British Isles' (ibid). Rees defines the four essential elements of Orwell's character: the rebel, a serious and tragic pessimist; the traditionalist, sympathetic to benign authority; the eighteenth-century rationalist, master of the plain style and the romantic, lover of the past. Rees affectionately portrays Orwell as an exceptionally sensitive man who took heroic measures to mortify himself, but who remained a calm, sensible, tough-minded, gentle-hearted individualist. He attributes Orwell's profound influence to his courage and truth-telling.

Julian Symons was introduced to Orwell at the socialist *Tribune* offices in 1944. A self-proclaimed Trotskyist, he had edited *Twentieth Century Verse* (1937-1939), served in the war, worked in advertising and began to write successful crime novels. After meeting him, Orwell publicly apologised for calling Symons 'a writer with Fascist tendencies' (p. 37). Orwell knew many leading authors in the compact London literary world. In 1944, for example, he had a congenial weekly lunch with his fellow journalists Symons, Anthony Powell and the talkative Malcolm Muggeridge.

ARTICLE

JEFFREY MEYERS

In 'Orwell: A reminiscence' (1963), Symons stressed Orwell's reticence about personal matters, his extreme integrity and honesty, his generosity and his blunt manner that almost amounted to gaucherie. Indulging in pop-psychology, he characterises Orwell as a man struggling to overcome childhood neuroses, and describes him as a libertarian socialist who upheld these principles in *Nineteen Eighty-Four*. He calls Orwell's talk 'a mixture of brilliant perception, common sense and wild assertion' (p. 38). Stressing his noble character, Symons 'believed that what Orwell wrote is less important than what he was' (p. 48). Always sympathetic to the oppressed, Orwell told Symons that he wanted to live near Blacks in the American South 'to experience directly what it felt like to be dispossessed and deprived' (p. 49).

George Woodcock's friendship with Orwell began with a vitriolic exchange in the American journal, *Partisan Review*, but Orwell had a chivalric sense of fair play and (as with Symons) recanted his unfair accusations. Anarchist, critic and editor, Woodcock was born in Canada, grew up in England and after the war returned to Canada to teach. He was impressed that Orwell could complete an almost perfect article straight on the typewriter. In *The Crystal Spirit*, (1966) he noted the shabby sahib's habitual outfit – 'old tweed sports coat, leather-patched at the elbows and baggy corduroys' (p. 7) – and gave a vivid account of his somewhat ravaged appearance:

> Orwell was a tall, thin, angular man, with worn Gothic features accentuated by the deep vertical furrows that ran down the cheeks and across the corners of the mouth. The thinness of his lips was emphasized by a very narrow line of dark mustache; it seemed a hard, almost cruel mouth until he smiled, and then an expression of unexpected kindliness would irradiate his whole face. The general gauntness of his looks was accentuated by the deep sockets from which his eyes looked out, always rather sadly (p. 3).

Woodcock noticed, in 1946, that when Orwell climbed the stone staircase to his flat on the top floor of the house on Canonbury Square, Islington, he was wheezing and gasping for breath by the time he reached the door. Woodcock agreed with the novelist John Wain: 'It was a tragic irony that the climate of Jura should have helped speed his death' (p. 43).

Anthony Powell, the handsome son of an army colonel and Orwell's younger contemporary at Eton, went up to Balliol College, Oxford. He worked in journalism and publishing, brought out his first novel in 1931 and served in the Intelligence Corps during the war. Powell became a close friend of Orwell after the war and found him, paradoxically, very assured but also very diffident. Explaining that personal affinity prevailed over political disagreements, Orwell told

Julian Symons that 'Tony is the only Tory I have ever liked' (Symons: 41).

Powell's 'George Orwell: A memoir' (1967) is the most vivid personal remembrance. The distinguished novelist describes Orwell as ascetic, intransigent, moralistic and difficult to know. Powell had no recollection of him at school, but Eton later became Orwell's bond with Powell, Connolly, Hollis, Rees and David Astor, the generous owner of the *Observer*. Powell captures Orwell's physical characteristics: his voice, carefully controlled not to sound 'public school'; his dreary steerage clothes and hairy ties. Powell describes his solemnity and persecution mania, his fondness for the Victorian atmosphere in places where he lived. He argues that since Orwell could function only in adversity he perversely needed to suffer on Jura.

Casting a rare light on Eileen, Powell recalls that she 'always appeared a little overwhelmed by the strain of keeping the household going, which could never have been easy. Possibly she was by temperament a shade serious for Orwell, falling in too easily with his own tendency to gloom' (p. 65). Powell saw Orwell in hospital towards the end of 1949 and 'it was fairly clear that he was not going to recover. Only the length of time that remained to him was in doubt' (p. 67). As James Boswell wrote of his tormented subject Samuel Johnson: 'He was afflicted with a bodily disease which made him often restless and fretful; and with a constitutional melancholy, the clouds of which darkened the brightness of his fancy, and gave a gloomy cast to his whole course of thinking' (Meyers: 182).

In 1971, Miriam Gross edited *The World of George Orwell* which included perceptive essays by Malcolm Muggeridge, William Empson and Michael Meyer. When Powell suggested an introduction to Muggeridge, Orwell – who had a violent streak – agreed but exclaimed: 'I shall probably sock him' (Meyers: 253). The son of a socialist politician, Muggeridge was educated at Cambridge. He was an anti-imperialist teacher in India and Egypt, a disenchanted communist in Moscow, a journalist in Calcutta and London, an ebullient paterfamilias and sexual philanderer. Orwell would have disapproved of Muggeridge's later incarnations as scourging editor of *Punch*, provocative television personality and (mocked as 'The Blessed Mugg') proselytising Catholic convert.

Like many others later on, Muggeridge attempts to press-gang Orwell for the Papists and body-snatch him for the political right. He claims that Orwell's passionate devotion to truth and distaste for compromise were akin to religious faith. He emphasises Orwell's contrariness and oddness, and asserts that he was deeply conservative. He describes Orwell's last illness, marriage to Sonia

JEFFREY MEYERS

Brownell, death and funeral. Muggeridge rejects Orwell's 'notion of himself as abnormally plain and unalluring. He was decidedly attractive to both men and women' (p. 169). When Orwell recalled the many absurdities of the propaganda at the BBC (where he worked from 1941-1943), 'he began to chuckle; a dry, rusty, growly sort of chuckle, deep in his throat, very characteristic of him and very endearing' (Meyers: 215).

Visiting Orwell in a sanatorium in February 1949, Muggeridge writes that they drank a bottle of rum hidden by Orwell, who was stoical about his suffering: 'I think he is fairly cheerful, but he said that the treatment he has to have is somewhat painful' (p. 294). In a famous formulation, Muggeridge noted that after his experience in the Spanish civil war, Orwell 'loved the past, hated the present and dreaded the future' (p. 172).

The influential poet and critic William Empson was born in Yorkshire, educated at Winchester and Magdalene College, Cambridge, where he was sent down after a servant discovered condoms in his room. In the 1930s he taught in Japan and China. The author of *Seven Types of Ambiguity* (1930), he worked with Orwell on the Eastern Service of the wartime BBC and gave drunken parties at his house in Hampstead.

Empson reports that during the war the over-scrupulous BBC paid Hitler a fee for broadcasting part of his speech. His narrative made Orwell come alive by quoting two of his famous remarks. Interviewing Indian propagandists for his programmes, Orwell loudly declared in his best Cockney accent: 'The FACK that you're black ... and that I'm white, has *nudding whadever to do wiv fit*' (p. 96). When Empson asked why Orwell was unhappy with the rave reviews of *Animal Farm*, he bitterly replied: 'Grudging swine, they are ... not one of them said it's a beautiful book' (p. 99).

Michael Meyer, born in London, the son of a Jewish timber merchant, was educated at Christ Church, Oxford. He later translated and wrote biographies of both Henrik Ibsen and August Strindberg. His excellent memoir (1971) emphasises Orwell's shyness, kindness, courtesy and wit – and his illuminating talk about politics. At their first meeting Meyer was 'surprised by his great height and thinness, his staring pale-blue eyes and his high-pitched drawl with its markedly Old Etonian accent' (p. 128). Like George Woodcock, Meyer notes that after a hurried walk when they were late for the theatre, 'the dreadful whistling heaviness of his breathing [lasted] for five or ten minutes after we had taken our seats' (p. 130). Proud of his carpentry, Orwell constructed an extremely uncomfortable chair and, after obtaining cherry wood, rare in wartime, criminally whitewashed it and made bookshelves without proper supports that curved like hammocks.

Meyer reports that several major publishers – Gollancz, Cape, Faber and Collins – turned down *Animal Farm* before it was eagerly taken by Fredric Warburg. He also recounts a ludicrous dinner in Orwell's flat in 1942 with H. G. Wells, who warned his host that he had stomach trouble and could not eat anything rich. He then tucked into two helpings of Eileen's spicy curry, topped up with two slices of rich plum cake. In lieu of a thank-you letter, Wells sent a furious message saying: 'You knew I was ill and on a diet, and deliberately plied me with food and drink' (p. 129).

Fredric Warburg, the publisher of *Animal Farm* and *Nineteen Eighty-Four*, was born into the family of Jewish financiers, educated at Westminster School and Christ Church, Oxford, and fought in the battle of Passchendaele in World War I. He describes Orwell, more critically than most, as 'a lonely man. He very rarely revealed anything personal about himself. … He was rather a chilly character … Orwell never liked being associated with anything that was too powerful or successful. … He wrote without regard to being popular and without fear of being detested' (Meyers: 173). In his memoir with the Orwellian title *All Authors Are Equal* (1973), Warburg, who had served in the wartime Home Guard with Orwell, recalls his author loading the wrong bomb into a training mortar with disastrous results: 'As the mortar, not being dug in, recoiled … Private Smith lost virtually all his front teeth top and bottom, while Private Jones was unconscious for at least 24 hours' (p. 38).

Warburg, who had published *Homage to Catalonia* in 1938, was very keen to acquire *Animal Farm* after several fearful and foolish publishers had rejected it. As he reaped all the benefits of Gollancz's earlier investment in Orwell, the sales of the satiric fable put his new firm on the map and propelled him beyond the dreams of avarice. He reports that 'very few books indeed have sold 9 million copies, even over a period of 28 years, and few of those few have been books of the highest quality' (p. 56). Warburg's report on *Nineteen Eighty-Four* notes the sado-masochism and unrelieved pessimism, and how the lyrical love affair of Winston and Julia intensifies the later horrors. The overwhelmingly grim novel, which lacked the style and wit of Orwell's animal fable, sold more than one million copies in Britain by 1972 and – with book clubs and paperbacks – more than nine million in America.

But – as Cyril Connolly observed – this surprising success came too late for Orwell to enjoy. Warburg writes that in February 1948 he visited Orwell in the sanatorium near Glasgow that looked more like an Arctic concentration camp than a place to cure tuberculosis. Warburg had the same grim impression as Muggeridge: 'He greeted me with a smile that was both welcoming and wintry. He told me he thought the antibiotic might be doing him a bit of good, but the actual injections, which seemed to him to be all too frequent, were exceedingly painful' (p. 99). Unfortunately, he had a severe reaction

ARTICLE

to an overdose of penicillin and could not tolerate the drug that might have saved his life.

Warburg's most penetrating comment came in his earlier book, *An Occupation for Gentlemen* (1960). He writes that Orwell risked his life unnecessarily – and often courageously – on duty in Burma, under fascist fire in Spain and when pursued by communists in Barcelona, during the Nazi bombing of London, in the perilous whirlpool off the coast of Jura and 'in his persistent neglect of elementary medical precautions. ... Obliteration was finally the sole remedy for his overpowering sense of guilt' (p. 234).

Jacintha Buddicom met Orwell's family in a Thames-side village in 1915 and maintained their friendship, corresponding when he was at Eton until he left for Burma in 1922. Her book, *Eric and Us: A Remembrance of George Orwell* (1974) is trivial, gossipy and superficial. Buddicom's extract in Miriam Gross's *The World of George Orwell* portrays his mother as vivacious, high-spirited and rather pretty, left-wing and with relatives who were militant suffragettes. According to Buddicom, his elderly, dour and discouraging father refused to pay for his university expenses and insisted that his son follow his own career in the Indian Civil Service. Eric and Jacintha, engaged in the usual childhood activities, kept pets and climbed trees, shot rats and rabbits, played tennis and croquet, swam and went fishing. She called him considerate and thoughtful, one of the kindest, most interesting and intelligent boys she knew.

Later on, Orwell's sister prudishly told Buddicom: 'I always found it strange that, although no hint of sex ever appeared in his conversation, his books were often quite lewd. This may have been a left over Victorianism inherited from our parents who never mentioned sex' (p. 131). Buddicom insists that their friendship was chaste: 'I never had a kiss from him and I didn't try to give him one' (Meyers: 12-13). But in a postscript to the posthumous 2007 reprint of her book, which clashes with Buddicom's innocent image, her cousin, Dione Venables, unconvincingly claims that Orwell proposed marriage while he was still at Eton and later attempted to rape her.

In his book *George Orwell* (1983), published in Japanese, Yasuharu Okuyama, Professor of English Literature at the prestigious Waseda University in Tokyo, included in English his 1980 interviews with Sir Steven Runciman and with F. A. S. (Adrian) Fierz. Runciman, Orwell's contemporary at Eton and later a distinguished historian of Byzantium and the Crusades, recalled how he was interested in Orwell's character and enjoyed the company of a boy who had read a lot of unusual books and liked showing off his knowledge: 'His mind worked in rather different ways, his reactions were different from the ordinary schoolboys' (p. 7). Runciman disliked Andrew

Gow at Eton – where he supervised Orwell's studies and taught him classics – and later on when they were colleagues at Cambridge. Gow did not like teenage boys and 'Eric was everything Gow couldn't understand. My sympathy is entirely for Eric' (p. 12).

Like Orwell's father, Gow discouraged him from going to university and he wound up, a rare Etonian, in the Burmese Police. Runciman thought it was quite a promising and well-paid job, and that Orwell was attracted to the unusual independence and authority of a colonial official. According to Runciman, Orwell 'had no intention of going to the university. … He wanted to go to the East' (p. 14). Orwell's pretending to be poor, Runciman thought, was not 'consciously dishonest, but it was all rather part of the legend about himself that he began to create, and which I think dates from when Burma went wrong' (p. 10).

The interview with Adrian Fierz was not nearly as rewarding as with Runciman. He was the son of Mabel Fierz, Orwell's patron. Married, she was also his lover, though Okuyama did not know this. Adrian recalls that Orwell took an interest in him and he was thrilled to spend time with the adventurous policeman from Burma. He introduced Adrian to some of his favourite books: *Gulliver's Travels,* the stories of Conan Doyle and P. G. Wodehouse. He took him to see *Hamlet* and to the British Museum, where he explained the exhibitions in the galleries. He remained fond of Adrian and attended his wedding in 1941.

The kind, gentle T. R. (Tosco) Fyvel, born in Cologne, was educated in Switzerland and at Cambridge, and emigrated to Palestine with his Zionist parents in the 1930s. During the war, he engaged in psychological warfare in North Africa and Italy. In 1945, he succeeded Orwell as literary editor of *Tribune* and then worked for the BBC. Fyvel wrote a perceptive memoir and, like Heppenstall and Runciman, felt Orwell helped create his own legend as a small-scale farmer, urban proletarian and sacrificial idealist. Though Orwell thought Zionists were unfair to the Arabs, he had many Jewish friends, including Koestler, Symons, Meyer, Warburg and Fyvel. Connolly, imitating Koestler's strong Hungarian accent, liked to ask: *'Ze great kvestion iss: "Who vill vin ze desert var? Wavell, Fyvel or Orvell?"'*

In his book, *George Orwell: A Personal Memoir* (1983), Fyvel records a rare personal revelation. Orwell confessed that, while on holiday in Marrakesh, Morocco, in 1938, he 'found himself increasingly attracted by the young Arab girls and the moment came when he told Eileen that he had to have one of these girls, on just one occasion. Eileen agreed and so he had his Arab girl' (p. 109). Orwell punctiliously asked if he could commit a single adultery and Eileen – who felt she had no choice – allowed him to go to a young prostitute. But it must have made her miserable and hurt their marriage. Fyvel, like Powell, found Eileen sickly and depressed: 'She seemed to sit in the garden sunk in unmoving silence while we talked. Mary, my wife, observed that Eileen not only looked tired and drawn but was drably and untidily dressed [despite having guests]. Trying in vain to involve Eileen in conversation, Mary said that she seemed to have become completely withdrawn' (p. 105).

Fyvel also recalls another grim and bitterly ironic incident. In September 1948, Orwell travelled from Jura to a hospital near Glasgow for a medical check-up. A commercial convention took place in the town, he had not reserved a room and 'had tramped from one full-up hotel to the next in heavy boots, carrying a suitcase weighted with purchases, finding a bed only when totally ill and exhausted' (p. 156). The debilitating trip to improve his health caused a relapse and sent him back to bed. The self-punishing Orwell always did everything the hard way.

Orwell's friends had to be careful when writing about Sonia, who lived until 1980. But everyone I interviewed for my biography thought she married the moribund Orwell for his literary fame and great wealth, which he could not spend and she did not share with Richard and Avril. None of the portraits is complete, but together they form a composite picture as his contradictory, complex and multifaceted personality takes shape, grows solid and springs into being. Orwell's reaction against wealthy upper-class Etonians turned him into an imitation proletarian, a lugubrious character whom his brother-in-law called 'gloomy George'. But he had shrewd political insight, even as a teenager, and became a literary and political genius on the anti-communist left.

Unlike most of his friends who had gone to university, Orwell – like Conrad, Hemingway and Malraux – gained experience in the world of action. He emerges from these accounts as guilt-ridden, self-punishing and austere, honest, idealistic and courageous. Though contentious and combative, he was greatly admired and died without enemies. Orwell's considerable disadvantages – years of abject poverty and incurable illness – make his literary achievement all the more impressive.

REFERENCES

Buddicom, Jacintha (1974) *Eric and Us: A Remembrance of George Orwell*, London: Leslie Frewin

Connolly, Cyril (1960 [1938]) *Enemies of Promise*, New York: Anchor

Dunn, Avril (1960) My brother, George Orwell, *Twentieth Century*, Vol. 169, March pp 255-261

Empson, William. (1971) Orwell at the BBC, Gross, Miriam (ed.) *The World of George Orwell*, London: Weidenfeld & Nicolson pp 94-99

Fyvel, T. R. (1982) *George Orwell: A Personal Memoir*, New York: Macmillan

Heppenstall, Rayner (1960) *Four Absentees*, London: Barrie & Rockliff

Hollis, Christopher (1956) *A Study of George Orwell*, Chicago: Henry Regnery

Koestler, Arthur (1955) A rebel's progress to George Orwell's death, *The Trail of the Dinosaur,* London: Collins pp 102-105

Meyer, Michael (1971) Memories of George Orwell, Gross, Miriam (ed.) *The World of George Orwell*, London: Weidenfeld & Nicolson pp 128-133

Meyers, Jeffrey (2000) *Orwell: Wintry Conscience of a Generation*, New York: Norton (I have cited other sources by these writers in my biography where they can all be found in one place.)

Muggeridge, Malcolm (1971) A knight of the woeful countenance, Gross, Miriam (ed.) *The World of George Orwell*, London: Weidenfeld & Nicolson pp 165-175

Okuyama, Yasuharu (1983) *George Orwell,* Tokyo: Waseda University Press pp 6-17, 18-25

Potts, Paul (1957) Don Quixote on a bicycle: In memoriam George Orwell, *London Magazine*, Vol. 4 pp 39-47

Powell, Anthony (1967) George Orwell: A Memoir, *Atlantic Monthly*, Vol. 220 pp 62-68

Rees, Richard (1962) *George Orwell: Fugitive from the Camp of Victory*, Carbondale: Southern Illinois University Press

Symons, Julian (1963) Orwell: A reminiscence, *London Magazine*, Vol. 9 pp 35-49

Warburg, Fredric (1973) *All Authors Are Equal*, New York: St. Martin's pp 7-15, 35-58, 92-120, 205-206

Woodcock, George (1966) *The Crystal Spirit: A Study of George Orwell*, Boston: Little, Brown

NOTE ON THE CONTRIBUTOR

Jeffrey Meyers has published four books on Orwell, including a biography in 2000. He has had thirty-three books translated into fourteen languages and seven alphabets, and published on six continents. He has recently published *Robert Lowell in Love* and *The Mystery of the Real: Correspondence with Alex Colville*, in 2016, and *Resurrections: Authors, Heroes – and a Spy* in 2018.

Barnhill: A Labour of Love

Norman Bissell, the author of *Barnhill*, a new novel about George Orwell's last years, explains how he came to write it on Luing, a neighbouring island of Jura, how he blended fact and fiction, the sources that inspired him and his original angles on the story.

WHY A NOVEL?

I can see a little of Jura from the cottage where I live in Cullipool village on the west coast of the Isle of Luing in Argyll. It lies directly to the south behind the triangular shaped Scarba and Barnhill is less than fifteen miles away – if the crow ever flew that way. I came to Luing in 2007 in order to write and live more fully, as did George Orwell on Jura, and hoped that lots of poems and essays would follow in this special slate island.

However, the more I thought about Orwell writing *Nineteen Eighty-Four* in his remote farmhouse the more I wanted to know what led him to write that book in such a spare, beautiful place. I was recovering from prostate cancer and starting to get involved in the work of the Isle of Luing Community Trust, but I couldn't get the question out of my head – what led Orwell to write his novel there? That was why I began to research his life and work and read as many biographies and memoirs of him as I could get my hands on, as well as his novels, essays, diaries and letters. Everything I came across fascinated me, from his essay 'Some Thoughts on the Common Toad' to his account of being *Down and Out in Paris and London*, from his 'As I Please' column in *Tribune* to *Homage to Catalonia*. I became almost as obsessed with Orwell as he was with warning the world of the dangers of totalitarian dictatorship. I felt a strong affinity with him, not just as a writer and democratic socialist, but as someone who loved these Inner Hebridean islands and the natural world of which we are part.

As a long-time advocate of geopoetics – the creative expression of the Earth in a fusion of arts, sciences and thinking – I was delighted to learn that Orwell had a great love for and knowledge of nature. His diaries contain details of the weather, plants, birds and other wildlife, and he had a deep longing for what he called the Golden Country, which was originally the Upper Thames part of Oxfordshire where he grew up. Winston Smith talks about it to Julia in the woods in *Nineteen Eighty-Four* and I believe Jura became his new Golden Country once he discovered it. He loved living on Jura and gave up his leases on the Stores at Wallington and his Islington flat because he intended to stay there for the rest of his life. The more I found out about his life and his desperate struggle to finish writing *Nineteen Eighty-Four* before his health failed, the more I realised that his tragic story could make a great feature film and novel. I felt that, rather than yet another non-fiction account, it deserved the widest possible audience and that a novel, in particular, would be the best way to try to explore his thoughts and feelings before and after the time when he was on Jura writing his most famous book.

As it happened, in April 2011 I came across an open call for proposals for screenplays to be developed by the Incubator scheme being funded by Creative Scotland under the auspices of a Scottish film production company, DigiCult Ltd. I submitted a pitch, a ten-page outline and a vision for a feature film about Orwell's last years and it was selected for development, along with five other proposals, by DigiCult's film producer Paul Welsh. Early in 2012 I was one of three writers who were commissioned to develop the screen story and script; he and I worked on it over the next two years and he is continuing to seek funding to take it forward and make the film.

In 2014, I applied for and was awarded a Creative Scotland artist's bursary to undertake research and professional development to write my first novel, partly based on the screenplay. Luath Press had published my poetry collection *Slate, Sea and Sky* in 2007 but I had never written a novel before and I sought professional advice on how to go about writing one. I attended novel writing courses at the Moniack Mhor Creative Writing Centre in the Highlands, at Ty'n y coed in North Wales and an Emergents novel editing course at Portree on Skye.

I also carried out research in the Orwell Archive at University College London and visited Orwell's former flat at Canonbury Square in Islington. It was smaller than I had imagined, the ceilings were lower and Orwell's writing and carpentry workroom was a lot narrower, but I had a much better picture of where he, his wife Eileen and baby son Richard lived at the end of the war. It turned out that the new owner of the flat was also writing a screenplay — for a horror film! Back on Luing I discovered that Donald Mackay, the creel fisherman who rescued Orwell, his son, nephew and niece in the Gulf of Corryvreckan after they almost drowned in 1947, came from the village of Toberonochy on Luing. Some Luineachs still remember him, Avril Blair and her husband Bill Dunn. Throughout these years I wrote my novel and finished it in early summer 2017.

In June 2018, I went to Barnhill with Richard Blair, his wife Eleanor and a large group of other members of The Orwell Society. At last I was inside the house I had imagined and written about for many years. I saw the kitchen with its Aga stove, admired his large free-

NORMAN BISSELL

standing bath upstairs and stood in the bedroom where he wrote most of *Nineteen Eighty-Four.* Amazingly, two parts of what was probably his motorbike were in the barn and were put together outside. I don't think the house had changed that much, it remained relatively spartan and I felt that there was still a strong sense of Orwell about the place. It was something of a relief that I found I didn't have to change much of what I'd written about the house.

FACT AND FICTION

The main challenge I found in writing a fictional account of Orwell's last years was to remain true to the central facts of his life whilst at the same time making the story as dramatic as possible. I felt that his relationship with Sonia Brownell from late 1945 until his death in January 1950 was crucial to this tragic love story and so I decided to write part of it from her point of view. There is a lack of information available about the contacts between them from April 1947 until she visited him in Cranham in May 1949. I found it surprising that there is only one letter from him to her in April 1947 and yet many love letters from him to Eleanor Jaques have recently turned up. Could it be that Sonia destroyed their correspondence to maintain their privacy? My response to this dearth of evidence was to have her visit him at Hairmyres Hospital in the summer of 1948 but to indicate that he was unsure whether she actually did so or he had imagined it. I suggested in a scene with Janetta Kee that there were strong psychological reasons for her decision to marry Orwell in 1949 rather than the unfair contention that she was simply out to benefit from his royalties. Of course, she did not write about her life with him as she was dying in November 1980, but I think this is legitimate poetic licence because her point of view is essential to the story and it's important to convey it as fully as possible.

Similarly, we know that Orwell spent two nights in Glasgow at New Year in 1946-1947 but nothing about where he stayed, what he did and whom he met. Knowing Glasgow as well as I do, I imagined him as a kind of inquisitive *flaneur* walking around the city centre, going on the subway to Gorbals and meeting folk in the Scotia Bar such as the writer Freddy Anderson who came to Glasgow from County Monaghan at that time. I wanted to show that Orwell was interested in working people and especially in the poor folk who slept in lodging houses and got their clothes in Paddy's Market by the River Clyde.

SOURCES OF INSPIRATION

My primary sources were Peter Davison's monumental *The Complete Works of George Orwell*, especially the last three volumes. Orwell's *A Life in Letters, Diaries, Essays* and *The Collected Novels* provided essential overviews of these key elements of his writing. The two books of interviews with people who knew Orwell which came out in 1984 were invaluable. *Orwell Remembered* by Audrey Coppard and Bernard Crick, and *Remembering Orwell* by Stephen Wadhams, recently re-issued as *The Orwell Tapes*, contained fascinating recollections by more than sixty people who knew Orwell and, in the latter case, hearing their actual voices was very revealing.

The memoirs by Tosco Fyvel, Richard Rees and George Woodcock provided significant insights into different aspects of the man with whom they were close friends. The selection from Malcolm Muggeridge's Diaries *Like It Was* and Fred Warburg's memoir *Some Authors Are More Equal Than Others* were also revealing in their own ways. The biographies of David Astor, Anthony Blunt, Arthur Koestler and Malcolm Muggeridge I read provided useful background but not much new information about their connections with Orwell.

The most detailed and perceptive secondary source I read was Gordon Bowker's biography *George Orwell* which greatly benefited from his access to Russian archives and previously unknown love letters. However, William Steinhoff's *The Road to 1984* and W. J. West's *The Larger Evils: 'Nineteen Eighty-four - the Truth Behind the Satire* were also particularly good on what led to Orwell's final novel and revealed his extensive knowledge of surveillance methods and the secret services.

Regarding Sonia, my main source was Hilary Spurling's *The Girl from the Fiction Department* which, although far from being a full biography, gave me valuable insights into Sonia's love of French culture, her attraction to the bohemian lifestyles of artists and useful indications about her character which I developed in my novel. I wrote to Hilary requesting an interview with her but she felt that all she had to say about Sonia was in her book. I learnt less than I expected about Sonia from David Plante's *Difficult Women* and found Michael Shelden's *Friends of Promise* more helpful in portraying Cyril Connolly and the world of *Horizon* than was his authorised biography of Orwell.

The American writer Jay Parini was an inspiration when it came to writing novels based on actual events in writers' lives, His novels on the last year in Leo Tolstoy's life and Herman Melville are outstanding and his fictional account of Walter Benjamin's sad end showed me how well it could be done. The only fictional take on part of Orwell's life I initially came across was David Caute's *Dr Orwell and Mr Blair* which focused on how Orwell came to write *Animal Farm*. Caute is an outstanding historian but I felt there was something lacking in his portrayal of Eric Blair.

The Orwell Society and its patron Richard Blair were also vital inspirations on account of their intimate knowledge of the man I was portraying and the important activities they offer which make

NORMAN BISSELL

us realise we're far from being alone in our interest in Orwell. The Society's website and social media posts are endless sources of new information about Orwell's life and work, as is the work of the Orwell Foundation.

Since *Barnhill* was published on 1 July 2019, I have found that there is considerable interest in Orwell in Scotland and this has been reflected in the many well-attended book launches and book festival talks I've given, in the questions asked at them – and in sales of the book.

ORIGINAL ANGLES ON THE ORWELL STORY

It seemed to me that another non-fiction book about this period in Orwell's life was not what was needed. Despite the millions of words he wrote and the millions more that have been written about him, the private man remains full of contradictions and something of an enigma. I felt that to understand what drove him so single-mindedly to write *Nineteen Eighty-Four* on Jura, and to pay the ultimate cost of doing so with his life, required the imaginative approach that only a novel can provide. At various points in the story I outlined his thoughts and feelings in the first person using a different font. After Eileen died, he had strong feelings of remorse and guilt over how he had treated her. And yet, so desperate was he to find another female companion and mother for his son, he recklessly proposed to a series of beautiful young women he hardly knew, with almost no chance of success.

I believe that my partial focus in the book on Sonia's doomed affair with the French philosopher Maurice Merleau-Ponty, her fascination with French culture and her modern attitudes to sexual relationships throws new light on her relationship with Orwell and her decision to marry him. I think judging her and him by present day mores and attitudes is a mistake.

I have also tried to show that Orwell was justified in being suspicious of David Holbrook's motives in visiting him at Barnhill and in carrying a gun in Paris and on Jura. The revelation by Gordon Bowker that the aptly named David Crook who spied on George, Eileen and the Independent Labour Party contingent fighting with the POUM on the Republican side in Spain, was trained by Ramon Mercador, later Leon Trotsky's assassin, indicates the danger that Orwell was in. It's quite likely that Stalin's NKVD (KGB) would do anything they could to stop Orwell finishing *Nineteen Eighty-Four* after the popular success of *Animal Farm*. This angle on the Orwell story led to prominent detailed, articles in the *Sunday Post*, the *Herald* and *Sunday National* in Scotland.

I believe I have also thrown new light on the mysterious visit by Andrew Gow to Orwell's UCH bedside just days before Orwell died which puzzled Bernard Crick. The art critic Brian Sewell was very close to Anthony Blunt and was convinced that Gow was also part of the Cambridge Soviet spy ring. When Sewell asked Blunt directly if this was the case he did not deny it. This suggests that Gow's visit was suspicious.

After I had finished my novel and it was to be published, it was quite a shock to learn that an Australian author Dennis Glover had also written a novel about Orwell's final years and that it would come out before mine. Perhaps this was not that surprising considering the significance of *Nineteen Eighty-Four* and Orwell's dramatic struggle to finish it. However, it was something of a relief when I read his book to find that our approaches to the story were very different. We met up at the UCL Orwell Conference in June 2019 and exchanged light-hearted experiences 'on the Orwell trail'.

My partner, Birgit, has asked me when will the ghost of George Orwell leave our house as the Alan Rickman character eventually did in the film *Truly Madly Deeply*. My answer so far has been 'Not for a while yet'. But I'm starting to wonder if he will ever leave us.

REFERENCES

Bowker, Gordon (2009 [2003]) *George Orwell*, London: Abacus

Bright-Holmes, John (ed.) (1981) *Like It Was: The Diaries of Malcolm Muggeridge*, London: Collins

Carter, Miranda (2002 [2001]) *Anthony Blunt: His Lives*, London: Pan Books

Caute, David (1995 [1994]) *Dr Orwell and Mr Blair*, London: Phoenix

Colls, Robert (2013) *George Orwell: English Rebel*, Oxford: Oxford University Press

Coppard, Audrey and Crick, Bernard (1984) *Orwell Remembered*, London: Ariel

Crick, Bernard (1981 [1980]) *George Orwell: A Life*, London: Penguin

Davison, Peter (1996) *George Orwell: A Literary Life*, Basingstoke: MacMillan Press

Davison, Peter (ed.) (2001 [1998a]) *Smothered Under Journalism 1946*, London: Secker & Warburg

Davison, Peter (ed.) (2001 [1998b]) *Our Job Is To Make Life Worth Living 1949-1950*, London: Secker & Warburg

Davison, Peter (ed.) (2002 [1998]) *It Is What I Think 1947-1948*, London: Secker & Warburg

Fyvel, Tosco (1983 [1982]) *George Orwell: a personal memoir*, London: Hutchinson

Glover, Dennis (2017) *The Last Man in Europe*, New York: Harry N. Abrams

Ingrams, Richard (1995) *Muggeridge: The Biography*, London: HarperCollins

Lewis, Jeremy (2016) *David Astor: A Life in Print*, London: Jonathan Cape

Meyers, Jeffrey 2001 (2000) *Orwell: Wintry Conscience of a Generation*, New York: W. W. Norton

Orwell, George (2011 [2010]) *A Life in Letters*, London: Penguin

Orwell, George (1984 [1933]) *Down and Out in Paris and London*, London: Penguin

Orwell, George (2000 [1938]) *Homage to Catalonia*, London: Penguin

Orwell, George (2000 [1976]) *The Complete Novels*, London: Penguin

NORMAN BISSELL

Orwell, George (2010 [2009]) *The Orwell Diaries*, London: Penguin
Orwell, George (1989 [1937]) *The Road to Wigan Pier*, London: Penguin
Orwell, Sonia and Angus, Ian (eds) (1971 [1968]) *The Collected Essays, Journalism and Letters of George Orwell, Vols I, 2, 3 and 4*, London: Penguin
Parini, Jay (1990) *The Last Station A Novel of Tolstoy's Last Year*, New York: Henry Holt and Company
Parini, Jay (1997) *Benjamin's Crossing*, New York: Henry Holt and Company
Parini, Jay (2010) *The Passages of H.M: A Novel of Herman Melville*, New York: Doubleday
Plante, David (1984 [1983]) *Difficult Women*, London: Futura
Powell, Anthony (1976) *To Keep the Ball Rolling, Vol. 1: Infants of the Spring*, London: Heinemann
Potts, Paul (1961) *Dante Called You Beatrice*, London: Readers Union, Eyre & Spottiswoode
Rees, Richard (1962 [1961]) *George Orwell: Fugitive From The Camp Of Victory*, Carbondale: Southern Illinois University Press
Rodden, John (1989) *The Politics of Literary Reputation: The Making and Claiming of 'St George' Orwell*, Oxford: Oxford University Press
Scammell, Michael (2010 [2009}) *Koestler: The Indispensable Intellectual*, London: Faber and Faber
Shelden, Michael (1995 [1989]) *Friends of Promise*, London: Minerva
Shelden, Michael (1992 [1991]) *Orwell: The Authorised Biography*, London: Minerva
Spender, Stephen (1978) *The Thirties and After*, Glasgow: Fontana Collins
Spurling, Hilary (2002) *The Girl from the Fiction Department: A Portrait of Sonia Orwell*, London: Hamish Hamilton
Steinhoff, William (1975) *The Road to 1984*, London: Weidenfeld and Nicolson
Taylor, D. J. (2003) *Orwell*, London: Chatto & Windus
Wadhams, Stephen (1984) *Remembering Orwell*, Ontario: Penguin Books
Wadhams, Stephen (2017) *The Orwell Tapes*, Ontario: Locarno Press
Warburg, Fredric (1973) *Some Authors Are More Equal Than Others*, London: Hutchinson
West, W. J. (1992) *The Larger Evils:* Nineteen Eighty-Four *the Truth Behind the Satire*, Edinburgh: Canongate Press
Williams, Raymond (1971) *Orwell*, London: Fontana/Collins
Woodcock, George (1984 [1967]) *The Crystal Spirit: A Study of George Orwell*, London: Fourth Estate

NOTE ON THE CONTRIBUTOR

Norman Bissell writes poetry, fiction, essays and reviews and is an experienced teacher, lecturer and performer. His publications include the poetry collection *Slate, Sea and Sky: A Journey from Glasgow to the Isle of Luing*, with photographs by Oscar Marzaroli (2007) and co-editing *Grounding a World: Essays on the work of Kenneth White* (2005). See www.normanbissell.com. He lives on the Isle of Luing in Argyll and is the Director of the trans-disciplinary Scottish Centre for Geopoetics and lead editor of its journal *Stravaig*. www.geopoetics.org.uk.

Leon Gellert, George Orwell and *Nineteen Eighty-Four*

Darcy Moore, a confessed bibliomaniac, tells the story of when he purchased what appeared to be a first edition of Orwell's dystopian masterpiece – both signed and at a knockdown price.

> As a child I lived in a home that was full of books. ... Rare works and first editions were kept under lock and key, and it took all my skill with a hairpin to gain entry to them.
>
> Leon Gellert

As an enthusiastic collector of books by George Orwell (1903-1950), the discovery that a signed first edition of *Nineteen Eighty-Four* (Orwell 1949) was on the market piqued my interest. The astronomical prices Orwell's inscribed books fetch nowadays has always prevented me owning such treasure, but it is fun to keep an eye on the excesses of the antiquarian book market.

Surprisingly, though out of my budget-range, the book was more affordable than anything signed I had spotted previously. The catalogue from the auction held in Melbourne, where the owner had successfully bid for the book some years ago, described 'item 164' as a 'first edition presentation copy signed by the author. Light green boards faded and soiled with minor spine damage. Fair condition' (Leski 2013).

Jeanette Winterson (2013) says book collecting is 'an obsession, an occupation, a disease, an addiction, a fascination, an absurdity, a fate. It is not a hobby. Those who do it must do it. Those who do not do it, think of it as a cousin of stamp collecting, a sister of the trophy cabinet, bastard of a sound bank account and a weak mind'. This is all undoubtedly true but, unfortunately, this collector does not possess a bank balance that could in any way be described as sound.

However, I made an offer for the novel, far below the asking price, under no illusion that the book would ever sit on my shelf. Surprisingly, unbelievably, my offer was accepted by the vendor who later said: 'I needed the money' when I asked why she sold such a treasure. The vendor's explanation made complete sense. She was selling other items at reduced prices and had a good record. I should just enjoy having procured a signed presentation copy of George Orwell's final, great novel at a bargain price. When it arrives in the mail, I can worry about it then.

Naturally enough, my first concern was the authenticity of the signature. Orwell rarely signed his books and when he did there was considerable variation in his handwriting, especially towards the end of his life when he was permanently confined to bed with pulmonary tuberculosis. Usually he signed as 'Geo. Orwell' but also as 'George Orwell' and occasionally as 'Eric Blair'. There are few known examples of him signing both his pseudonym and birth name in the same book.

I contacted the auction house and they confirmed the previous sale and the authenticity of the item. They did not respond to a supplementary email asking how they had confirmed that authenticity. Fair enough, it was some time ago.

RESEARCHING LEON GELLERT

Who was Leon Gellert anyway and how had he managed to have his copy of the great novel signed? Orwell was in the hospital at University College London when the book was released. He loved his Biro pen which made it easier for him to write while horizontal in bed. There were 25,575 copies of *Nineteen Eighty-Four* printed in the UK during June 1949 and he did sign some at this time for hospital staff (Fenwick 1998: 132). One of these sold recently for US $26 500 (Abe Books 2019).

While waiting for a carefully wrapped, tracked package to arrive in the mail, I started researching Leon Gellert (1892-1977). He was an Australian poet, literary editor, columnist and survivor of the ill-fated Gallipoli campaign. How could I have never heard of him before? It all made sense though. Orwell would have related to this returned serviceman, poet and journalist.

Gavin Souter had authored a biography of Gellert in 1996 which had only 270 copies printed but was now available to download. I started reading and stayed up late. *A Torrent of Words* was well-written and Gellert was proving an interesting subject in his own right. Souter, who worked contemporaneously at the media company Fairfax with his subject, described the middle-aged journalist as:

> Strongly built, with an urbane but occasionally testy demeanour, and incisive tone of voice, he usually wore a dark suit, a homburg and black-rimmed spectacles. To me he looked like a middle-aged company director who probably belonged to Tattersalls or the Imperial Services Club (Souter 1996: 1-2).

The 'curmudgeonly' Gellert had a surprisingly bohemian friendship with one of Australia's most famous artists, Norman Lindsay. This began in 1917 when Lindsay had illustrated Gellert's war poetry, ensuring strong sales. Souter tells the story of the first time the two met in person. Recognising Lindsay at a museum from photographs, Gellert introduced himself and 'the slender artist seized the sturdier poet around his waist and the two of them danced between glass cases in a transport of joy' (ibid: 18). One assumes they had corresponded beforehand.

The pair patronised city haunts with bohemian friends during the 1920s; coffee at Mockbell's, wine at Pelligrini's. Lindsay's home, in the Blue Mountains at Springwood, was a popular destination for these friends between the wars. There were a number of ghostly encounters at the property, along with other shenanigans. Souter explains that Lindsay, being 'psychically hyperactive', was fond of the Ouija board and 'communicated with his dead soldier brother' although his friend was sceptical. Gellert was reported to have had terrible nightmares while staying in the Lindsay household, which the artist assumed 'were after-effects of having been shell-shocked' rather than participation in his séances' (ibid: 28).

Gellert, who was a schoolteacher, built a career editing journals such as *Home* and *Art in Australia* rather than writing verse. From 1947, freed from the demands of sub-editing, making up pages and dealing with contributors, Gellert began writing for Fairfax. Souter believed that Gellert's public reputation was made by the poems written during the Great War but later in his life was 'generally regarded as the *Herald*'s most graceful writer' (ibid: 2).

Souter titled his biography – *A Torrent of Words* – after the first instalment of Gellert's long-lived weekly newspaper column, 'Something Personal'. The piece discussed lexicographer Eric Partridge in 'an elegant, ironic, sometimes arch and sometimes grumpy style that soon became a familiar part of Saturday's *Herald*'. Later entitled 'Speaking Personally', these columns continued until retirement from Fairfax in 1961 (ibid: 55).

I was hoping these pieces would remind me of George Orwell's 'As I Please' column published in the leftist newspaper, *Tribune*, between 1943 and 1947. Gellert had been popular enough to warrant the publication of two book-length collections of his columns, *Week After Week* (1953) and *Year After Year* (1956). There had been tragedy at the height of Gellert's success when his only daughter died losing her baby during childbirth in 1954 (ibid: 52).

I wondered if Souter were still alive. He would be quite elderly. Online he was listed as the patron of the Mosman Historical Society and contact was soon made. We chatted on the phone. Souter, now aged 90, lives in Mosman, the suburb where Gellert resided. Gavin kindly invited me to his place for further discussions about Orwell and how the inscribed book had come into Gellert's possession. He was intrigued too.

MORE RESEARCH NEEDED

Did Gellert travel to England between June and December 1949? There was no hint of this in Souter's book nor could I find any passenger records online. The sources Souter listed were almost all held at the State Library of New South Wales, including a will. Perhaps I could find some indication that Gellert had made the journey to London? Maybe he visited Orwell in the hospital at University College London? I phoned the Mitchell Reading Room and reserved his papers to read on the weekend.

When the book arrived, it was in better than fair condition with the usual leaning spine, so commonly found with Orwell's books printed during the 1930s and 1940s. It was undoubtedly a UK first edition, published by Secker & Warburg in June 1949 and the inscription was convincing, although Orwell's signature, written in black Biro, was subtly different from others I have seen. He was near death. It did cross my mind that Orwell's much-loved Biro was blue, so I checked Peter Davison's magisterial twenty-volume *Complete Works of George Orwell*, and the only mention was of a 'blue-black' or 'blue' Biro. I made a mental note that the *Oxford English Dictionary* records Orwell's letter of 2 January 1948 as the first recorded use of 'Biro' in print (*CWGO* 15: 360).

Saturday dawned and I caught the train to Sydney to research and meet Souter. Spring sun beamed into the Mitchell Library Reading Room via the stained-glass windows as a satisfyingly full trolley of Gellert's papers awaited my perusal. Photographs, clippings, letters, his will and a trove of goodness knows what awaited on microfilm.

I opened the first folder. Gellert's columns for Fairfax were carefully preserved and annotated with the date and publication. My excitement grew as I flicked through his journalism dating back almost 70 years. I quickly had a Eureka moment which fuelled my growing anticipation.

In his 'Something Personal' column for 27 March 1954 was a piece entitled 'Nationalism according to Orwell'. It was a review of Orwell's posthumous collection of essays, *England my England*. I love how Gellert describes Orwell as 'a natural mutineer'. Gellert's attitude to Orwell was a little ambivalent and he posits that 'none of us will come to any harm reading his ruthless "Notes on nationalism"'. It is an intelligent and perceptive review which concludes asking the questions: 'Are YOU a nationalist? And for that matter, am I? And what of George Orwell himself?' (Gellert 1954).

'LEND A BOOK, LOSE A FRIEND'

After almost an hour of reading, a column in the *Sun-Herald* for 3 April 1960 made me start. 'Lend a book, lose a friend' confirmed that both Gellert and his father were passionate, 'inveterate bibliophiles' (Gellert 1960). It is best to let Gellert take up the story:

> As a child I lived in a home that was full of books. ... Rare works and first editions were kept under lock and key, and it took all my skill with a hairpin to gain entry to them.
>
> My father was an inveterate bibliophile ... after the day's work, he was combing the bookshops for treasure. At least once a week he would come home laden with booty and, avoiding my mother's disapproving eye, stow it away in his study until such a time as he might examine it at leisure.
>
> And in all that vast collection there was not a dog-eared page or a grimy finger mark. At the end of his days, every book in his library looked as though it had just come from the publishers.

I felt a strong kinship with the bibliomania of the Gellerts and was pleased to have begun trawling through his papers with this thick folder of newspaper clippings. I read on:

> Although he was generous to a fault in other respects, he never lent his books. To protect himself against the wiles of the borrower, he employed some rather cunning ruses.
>
> When visitors expressed a wish to borrow a work which had taken their fancy, he would quote the whole of Polonius' advice to Laertes, laying special emphasis on the line which deals with the loss of friendship following a loan. This was known as the 'Shakespearean manoeuvre'.
>
> If they survived the recital and still persisted in their request, he resorted to what we termed the 'Philanthropic formula'. With the beaming smile of one who would sacrifice his last drop of blood to save the life of a fellow mortal he would say: 'I'll make you a present of it. Maybe in the course of time and by exhaustive searching, I shall be lucky enough to find another copy to replace it.'

I chortled: what an amusing and delightful anecdote about his father's eccentricities. Gellert goes on to say that these ploys never worked for him as he usually misquotes Shakespeare terribly and due 'to the low state that common courtesy had fallen' since his father's days friends jump at the chance to score a new book for free forcing him to develop a new 'dodge which [will] enable me to retain the more contemporary works in my library'.

DARCY MOORE Gellert explained his ingenious response to friends who wished to borrow a book from his library:

> 'Well, old man, I'd rather you didn't,' I would reply. 'It's a presentation copy from the author, as you can see, and I just don't like letting it out of my hands, even for a moment. Sorry, old man.' It was a treat to watch his face as he read the inscription on the flyleaf. ... Every book in my possession that had been written since I came of age bore its personal message from the author, and furnished me with an excuse for not lending it.

My good humour and lightness of heart, sitting in that heritage-listed sandstone reading room where Gellert undoubtedly spent many quality hours, soured. Several silent expletives followed as I sat and digested that Gellert was admitting to faking signatures, especially with his contemporary first editions. That must include *Nineteen Eighty-Four*. He didn't know Orwell personally. He wasn't in London in 1949. I read on:

> Some of the descriptions were long and effusive but most were brief and to the point: 'To L.G., the old blighter – with all my affection, Bertrand Russell'; 'To L.G., with abiding homage, W. Somerset Maugham'; To L.G. In appreciation. What about popping over here and getting stinko together, F. Scott Fitzgerald,' etc. etc.

You really had to laugh. This was a great anecdote and even though I was disappointed at the reality, that my expensive purchase was not what it purported, it was a wonderful story. Gellert was often very creative inscribing admiring messages to himself from the good and the great including the poet John Masefield, H. G. Wells and Evelyn Waugh. Masefield acknowledges his verse 'is not up to your standard' and that 'I just live for your cheery notes' and Wells congratulates Gellert 'on that thing of yours in the *Manchester Guardian*! The best of its kind I've read for many a day'.

Gellert really hams it up describing how vastly amused he is by friends and colleagues who visibly 'tremble with veneration' on seeing how well-acquainted he was with the literary giants of his generation which he shrugs off by explaining, 'in my game, one just meets them and that's that'.

CAVEAT EMPTOR

Walking out of the Mitchell Reading Room feeling more than a little melancholy, my phone pinged: it was an email from the auction house. They must have added my name to their distribution list. I clicked on the phone number and spoke with an employee who listened to my tale. I asked her what their policy was for situations like this when they had sold an item that was not authentic. The Boss, she said, would call me back next week.

It turned out that the Auction House did not really do any checking of the authenticity of this item as they were selling a comprehensive collection of signed letters and books amassed by Austrian-born Fred Goldschlager, a well-known Australian collector of autographs. He died in 2013 and his family were auctioning his estate. I do wonder how he came to possess Gellert's copy of *Nineteen Eighty-Four*? I also wonder what other books from Gellert's library are in the marketplace as 'signed, presentation copies'?

Mercifully, it was some time after all this that I realised Gellert had published 'Mankind Is doomed', a glowing review of *Nineteen Eighty-Four*, in the *Sydney Morning Herald* on 23 July 1949. It would have certainly convinced me it was a signed copy and made the realisation that Orwell had not inscribed the book even more disappointing. Gellert could not have been more fulsome in his praise of the novel in his review, saying:

> I have just finished reading what must surely be a masterpiece of modern fiction ... ring up your bookseller and order a copy (Gellert 1949).

I had elatedly bought the book on a Saturday. One week later, I knew it was not signed by Orwell. However, I do feel richer for the experience of learning about Leon Gellert and meeting Gavin Souter. In the back of my mind I wondered if having the story published would increase the price of the book, inscribed by that wit Leon Gellert, especially if I had it printed in his old newspaper, the *Sydney Morning Herald*?

Perhaps, Dear Reader, you would like to pick-up a first edition of *Nineteen Eighty-Four*, in fair condition, with a fascinating local association? Although, I am not at all certain I wish to sell it.

REFERENCES

AbeBooks.com (2019) The most expensive signed books ever sold on AbeBooks. Available online at https://www.abebooks.com/books/rarebooks/10-signed-books.shtml, accessed on 1 October 2019

Fenwick, Gillian (1998) *George Orwell: A Bibliography*, New Castle, Delaware and London: Oak Knoll Press & St. Paul's Bibliographies

Gellert, Leon (1949) Something Personal: Mankind is doomed, *Sydney Morning Herald*, 23 July. Available online at https://trove.nla.gov.au/newspaper/article/18123221, accessed on 15 October 2019

Gellert, Leon (1954) Something Personal: Nationalism according to Orwell, *Sydney Morning Herald*, 27 March. Available online at https://trove.nla.gov.au/newspaper/article/18416882, accessed on 1 October 2019

Gellert, Leon (1960) Lend a book lose a friend, *Sun-Herald*, 3 April. Available online at http://smharchives.smedia.com.au/Olive/APA/freesearch/get/image.ashx?kind=preview&href=SMH%2F1960%2F04%2F03&page=108&ext=png, accessed on 1 October 2019

Leski Auctions Catalogue (2013) *Sporting & Historical Memorabilia*, Melbourne, 14 & 15 August, Mossgreen Pty. Ltd.

DARCY MOORE

Orwell, George (1949) *Nineteen Eighty-Four*, London: Secker & Warburg

Orwell, George (1998) *Two Wasted Years: The Complete Works of George Orwell, Vol. XV*, Davison, Peter (ed.) London: Secker & Warburg

Souter, Gavin (1996) *A Torrent of Words*, Canberra: Brindabella Press

Winterson, Jeanette (2013) *Art Objects: Essays on Ecstasy and Effrontery*, New York: Knopf Doubleday Publishing Group

NOTE ON THE CONTRIBUTOR

Darcy Moore is a deputy principal at a secondary school in New South Wales. He teaches English and History and has worked as an academic in post-graduate teacher education at the University of Wollongong. His interest in Orwell began at school, thirty-six years ago, when he was enthralled by *Animal Farm* and *Nineteen Eighty-Four*. He is currently working on a book, *Orwell in Paris*. He blogs at *darcymoore.net* and his Twitter handle is @Darcy1968. His Orwell collection can be accessed at darcymoore.net/orwell-collection/.

1984 in 2020: The Deeper Concerns

Although the quantity and penetration of current global surveillance would make Orwell blush, the deeper issues would make him scowl. Is 'truth' the greatest casualty of the 21st century? asks Tom Cooper.

THE STATE OF THE PLANET

It was amusing to read recently in a major newspaper that there are more than 10,000 hidden cameras in Manhattan. Why was I amused? Because if the cameras are *hidden*, how can one be sure there are not 20,000 or 100,000 of them? After all, millions of Manhattan citizens and visitors carry cameras hidden in plain sight on their cell phones.

Add to this the satellites overhead, the Trojan horses and cookies detecting these words that you read, the security cameras in virtually all buildings and the medical cameras inside your body during surgery. Given that there are underwater, blimp, drone, hotel, highway, police, hospital, mall and automobile 'cams' everywhere, am I even more likely to be observed than Winston Smith?

Winston hoped for some 'off camera' hideaway where he could write in a confessional mode in his journal about his 'thoughtcrime'. But he was never sure if he had found an oasis of privacy, even when he was 'alone' with his lover Julia and with the 'proles'. In this age when the e-terrorists with ransomware say they are spying on us through our webcams, how may I be sure that I am any more invisible to third parties than Winston was … even as I write these words with my webcam supposedly 'off'?

Where there are cameras, there may well be microphones *and* recording devices *and* links to global voyeurs. So who can be sure which of my spoken words are recorded and transmitted globally and where my image might next be broadcast or altered?

THE ISSUES

Hence much of the anxiety of *Nineteen Eighty-Four* is widely available in 2020. And the issues of media-government relations also currently abound. Although billions of earth dwellers do not have access to the 'wired world' due to the 'digital divide', nevertheless, within the half of the world which is 'tech dominant',

TOM COOPER

numerous Orwellian issues persist. In a list I made of such issues, I have labelled eleven as important and four more as 'terminal tendencies'. Those eleven which are secondary I have called:

1) ubiquitous surveillance;
2) centralised, hierarchic media;
3) media as catalysts to toxic emotions and violence;
4) dehumanisation;
5) mechanical substitute patterns for intimate, personal relationships;
6) formulaic, mindless disposable culture;
7) easily censored, intercepted, doctored or faked correspondence and documentation;
8) the mediated routinisation of leisure time;
9) electronic racial and national profiling and hate speech;
10) the devaluation of intuitive and critical thinking in favour of group e-opinion including (anti-) social media;
11) global indoctrination (such as through advertising).

While these issues could call for endless elaboration, to some degree many of them already have been a focus for discussion. So let us go deeper.

THE DARKER ISSUES

The issues above point deeper and darker into what may be Orwell's greatest concerns … no less dangerous and relevant in 2020 than during the late 1940s when he penned his dystopian masterpiece. These deeper issues might be called:

1: Media addiction and the end of pluralism: as just one example we are told that English-speaking citizens will absorb four years of advertising via screens in a life-time. Despite the feigned pluralism of over one thousand channels and millions of advertisments, there is only one monolithic message programmed into audiences from cradle to grave: 'There is something wrong with you. Buy something.' There are now media addiction centres worldwide although most addicts will not use them. Mind control, albeit often veiled, is persistent.

2: Media authority: audiences have strong opinions about say Putin, Johnson, Kim and Trump in politics and Lady Gaga, Elton John and Beyoncé in pop culture. We talk as If we understand celebrities, world issues and leaders as if we personally know them. Yet how few of us have actually spent eight hours with any of these people off-camera and off-script? The media provides a false sense of 'knowing' and has become in a sense the 'new epistemology'. We accept and chronically emit pseudo-knowledge.

3: The one-sidedness of communication: despite the illusion of interactivity, world leaders, global corporations, advertisers, entertainment conglomerates and others constantly force-feed iterated messages evoking the spirit of propaganda, mass programming and product dependency. While communication is rumoured to be two-way or multi-channel, ultimately world audiences are told and sold what to do and buy.

4: The destruction of reality, language, human dignity and truth: for Macbeth's witches 'fair is foul, foul is fair'. And for Orwell and the current era 'fake is true, true is fake'. Not only is trust in 'truth' destroyed but the very language which describes it is also reversed as with Orwell's 'newspeak'. Without a sense of reality and standards of truth-telling, humans lose trust in public discourse. We become adrift in amoral waters with little sense of personal worth. Just as Winston is chronically craving a sense of knowing what is *truly* true, the 21st century is pocked by those constantly aspiring to topple false gods, the authors of newspeak. But are we also trapped inside a cocoon of false knowing … like Winston?

THE ANTIDOTE

What can possibly be done if Orwell does not seem so much past as future? What if the instruments of surveillance are now carried routinely in the purses and pockets not only of Big Brother, but also Big Sister, Mother, Father, Daughter, Cousin and Son? What if the prophesies of the end of privacy, reality, accountability and truth as we know them soon seem irreversible? What is the antidote?

Educators will always say that we need more and better education. Political advocates will argue that we must be better citizens, vote knowledgably and remain concerned. Spiritual leaders will call for more prayer and inner work. Global organisations such as the UN will ask for unified action in areas such as sustainability and peace. Artists will proclaim that a 'people without art is like a planet without atmosphere'. Ethicists often call for more codes and policies.

All of these are right in their way and we need all approaches to make certain there is a united effort. But the key to personal liberation from persistent and pernicious programming lies within. What suffers most in *Nineteen Eighty-Four* is thinking which becomes cloned, feeling which becomes artificial and action which is routinely homogenised.

TOM COOPER

The antidote, then, must come from a different direction. The ultimate call is for action which is enlightened, feeling which is genuine and thinking which is creative and independent in the service of humanity. The antidote for 2020 is hidden in the number. We need 20/20 critical vision to see through the programming, the propaganda and the pseudo-intelligence.

To paraphrase Shakespeare's Cassius, 'the fault is not in our surveillance … but in ourselves'. So too is the antidote.

NOTE ON THE CONTRIBUTOR

Professor Tom Cooper, of Emerson College, taught at Harvard, where he graduated *magna cum laude*, and was recently an 'ethics expert' at a United Nations project in Vienna and Athens. A former assistant to Marshall McLuhan, he was a consultant to the Elders Project which involved Nelson Mandela, Kofi Anan and Jimmy Carter. Cooper is a playwright with a PhD in theatre and media, a union musician who trained at the Royal Conservatory, poet, black belt, blogger and author of eight books and more than two hundred academic and professional articles and reviews.

REVIEWS

Dzhordzh Oruell: Biografiya [George Orwell: Biography]
Masha Karp
Vita Nova, St Petersburg, 2017, pp 608
ISBN: 978 5 93898 642 8 (hbk)

The work under review — a fine, comprehensive biography of Orwell — suggests that the writer, in the works for which he is best known, mediated between Russian/Soviet culture on the one hand and Western culture on the other, performing a critical act of translation from one political culture into another. Orwell also performed an act of warning, regarding first fascism and then the totalitarian world of Soviet communism. Orwell proved to be well-suited for the role. Karp astutely captures the Russian Orwell, his uniquely Russian sensibility among British writers and his skill in rendering distinctly Russian politics in a totalitarian state.

Karp herself is a respected translator of one culture into another. She has translated into Russian, among others, works by W. H. Auden, Dylan Thomas, Virginia Woolf and Tom Stoppard. For nearly 20 years, she worked for the Russian Service of the BBC. The anglophone reader of Russian feels at times like an eavesdropper on a conversation between the anglicised author and her Russian readership. For example, Karp notes that in 1946, while already working on *Nineteen Eighty-Four*, Orwell suggested to the BBC that he do a piece on Pontius Pilot, 'or an imagined conversation between Pontius Pilot and, let's say, Lenin' (p. 493). Karp observes wryly: 'Orwell could in no way know that in Russian, a novel about Pontius Pilot had already been written' (p. 493). Mikhail Bulgakov's *Master and Margarita* did not see the light of day for another two decades, it should be added.

Karp argues that, with *Nineteen Eighty-Four*, Orwell shows how acutely he discerned the Soviet experience to recount with accuracy not only the externals of daily life but also to reveal the inner world of those existing under the repressive regime of Big Brother. She says of Orwell's achievement:

> [His] acquaintance even with the smallest details of daily life [made] it difficult to believe that [*Nineteen Eighty-Four*] was written by a person who had never been to the USSR … But [more impressively] Orwell created the internal life of Winston Smith exclusively by dint of his own imagination, literary talent

and many years of growing accustomed to a world far from his own (p. 494, reviewer translation).

She notes that Orwell got it right, even down to 'the lift eternally in disrepair' (p. 494). Ease and efficiency were never part of Soviet life, nor part of the imagined world of *Nineteen Eighty-Four*. Karp points out, however, that Orwell had ample examples from which to draw. She cites as influences on *Nineteen Eighty-Four* works by Swift, Wells, Kipling, Chesterton, the literature of the 1930s and 1940s 'on humanity vs. Fascism' (p. 498), as well as Charlie Chaplin (p. 350). Most significant of all, she argues, was Zamyatin's *We* (1923) which he read in French, called to his attention by the literary historian Gleb Struve, son of Lenin's early rival Peter Struve, along with Aldous Huxley's dystopian novel of 1932, *Brave New World* (p. 498). Appropriately, both cultures between which Orwell mediated provided him with dystopian inspiration for *Nineteen Eighty-Four*.

On the other hand, however effectively Orwell made Soviet totalitarianism comprehensible in the West, Karp herself missteps in her translation of Orwell into Russian. Orwell's phrase 'Big Brother' captures the essential lie at the heart of the regime. 'Big Brother' suggests a protector, a benevolent figure and member of one's own family, capable even of replacing one's parents. The words also imply the absence of hierarchy in the form of birth order, rather equality among siblings. There may be the relinquishment of agency in return for protection but otherwise one's big brother offers security, affirming shared familial membership. The world of *Nineteen Eighty-Four* puts the lie to all that with painful irony.

Karp uses the phrase 'Starshiy Brat' – that is, older/senior brother, for 'Big Brother'. The irony of Orwell's phrase has disappeared, as has the implication that black is white and white is black in *Nineteen Eighty-Four*. Karp's phrase is redolent of hierarchy, superiority, preference. Gone is Orwell's sense that language has been turned on its head. Karp, I believe, should reconsider her rendering of a phrase that embodies the central tenets of the novel and perhaps, in revising the work, employ the direct translation, 'Bol'shoy Brat'.

The chapter on Orwell's time in Spain, while sufficient in its historical narrative for a biography on Orwell, is nonetheless somewhat disappointing. The author relies on standard English language works of scholarship on the Spanish civil war such as Radosh et al., *Spain Betrayed: The Soviet Union in the Spanish Civil War* (2001) and Antony Beevor, *The Battle for Spain: The Spanish Civil War, 1936-1939* (2006). Karp does use NKVD documents to be found on the internet. She has examined other unpublished sources, but they are ones located in the collection of the International Brigade Memorial Trust in the Marx Memorial Library in London. Unlike the internet documents, they are not ones that would be readily accessible to Karp's Russian readership, but certainly available to Western scholars. It is unfortunate that she did not consult the extensive holdings on the Spanish civil war to be found in the former Communist Party archive (Moscow) known by the acronym RGASPI. This reviewer has found that archive to be one of the more open of the former Soviet archives, although in the past decade such access has been growing increasingly problematical. Use of that archive would have elevated the value of the work under review, certainly making it a candidate for translation into English.

Overall, the author relies on standard published sources, including Orwell's correspondence as well as standard works of Western scholarship as noted in her account of the Spanish civil war. Missing, yet exceedingly desirable, is the Russian scholarship on Orwell. Those debates and discussions are absent from the work under review, yet even a summary account of that material would contribute to Western scholarship on Orwell, strengthening the argument for Orwell as a cross-cultural figure. But Karp may have believed such material of less interest to her Russian readership than the Western sources she relies on.

Regrettably, the work lacks a bibliography. A listing of major Russian works on Orwell would also be a first step towards making them accessible to a larger audience and add to the case for translation of the work under review. Karp's biography is part of a series produced by the St Petersburg publisher, Vita Nova, devoted to the lives of 'the greatest figures past and present'. Orwell is one of several writers, both Russian as well as English, in the series. In sum, Karp's contribution to the series is a solid, comprehensive biography based on Western scholarship designed for the Russian reader already familiar with Orwell's major works. A translation would offer little that is new to the Western scholar or to students of Orwell other than a full overview of his life based on already familiar and well-known sources.

Alexis Pogorelskin,
University of Minnesota Duluth

Sur les Traces de George Orwell
Adrien Jaulmes
Equateurs, Paris, 2019, pp 157
ISBN 978 2 84990 635 4 (pbk)

In 1984, *Le Monde* did a feature on *Nineteen Eighty-Four*. I was living in Paris at that time and had never read anything about Orwell written with so much respect. Increasingly captivated by this suddenly towering international figure, I started avidly reading his works. The new and enticing Penguin edition was available at W. H. Smith on Rue de Rivoli. Adrien Jaulmes writes for the *Figaro*, which I never read, supposing it to be a sinister Gallic equivalent of the *Telegraph*. But it is a pleasure to find that familiar tone of puzzled admiration coming through in his excellent work, as well as that exciting sense of timeliness. Of course, as he stresses, it isn't the Soviet Union we are worried about now but the current ubiquity of digital surveillance, disinformation and coercive devices. The telescreens, with the unlimited opportunities for enslavement that they offer, are everywhere. 'George Orwell did try to warn us,' says former *Guardian* editor Alan Rusbridger in conclusion to his overview of the present surveillance scene in today's *Times Literary Supplement* (25 October 2019).

The plan of this short book is to track Orwell's itinerary as a writer by visiting the places where he worked. The aim is to understand what the author calls his 'almost paranormal' understanding of totalitarianism. Doing it in a journalistic way rather than academically, Jaulmes starts with a visit to Eton and dwells with relish on the paradoxes he finds there. Orwell hated cliques and schools but seems to have liked Eton, socialist though he was, because it encouraged the boys think for themselves. In fact, he eventually did so well at thinking for himself that he has come to be seen as a model pupil, with a bronze bust of him adorning the premises. Yet if there was one thing Orwell hated even more than cliques it was model pupils, of whom he produces a gruesome array in *Nineteen Eighty-Four*. He found the Victorian classic, *Eric, or Little by Little*, on how to be good at school, particularly nauseating. It was one of his incentives for using his pseudonym.

Watching the boys milling about in their quaint outfits 'like penguins on an ice-flow', learning about the Ball Game and other arcane rituals, Jaulmes finds the whole set-up rather Freemason-like. It produces a kind of brotherhood of members who can quickly recognise one another by signs unknowable to non-members. This has distinctly ominous connotations, as Winston Smith discovers when he starts dreaming of a secret brotherhood that could save the world. The Frenchman notes that both David Cameron and Boris Johnson are old-Etonians, but does not venture to draw conclusions for our present plight.

Impressively, he goes all the way from Windsor to Mawlamyaing (formerly Moulmein) and Katha to see where Orwell's first novel *Burmese Days* (1933) was coming from, and what doing 'the dirty work of the Empire' must have been like. Orwell's hands-on working knowledge of how to keep people down comes across as a key to his lucidity about modern dictatorship. His experiences are well summarised and that piece of the puzzle falls neatly into place. With their long experience of oppressive rule, locals remind Jaulmes that Orwell wrote three books about Burma: *Burmese Days, Animal Farm* and *Nineteen Eighty-Four*.

Back on home ground, we see how his self-imposed destitution in London and Paris completes his basic training in oppression. It adds the opposite point of view: that of the powerless – of the animals who are not pigs in *Animal Farm*, and of Winston, the last man, in *Nineteen Eighty-Four*. For someone with such strong material to write about and so much determination to be a writer, it took Blair the apprentice a long time to become Orwell the master. Without support from the old boy network he would almost certainly not have made it. Even with it, he had not got very far during his first nine years on that rugged road. When he turned north in early 1936 to gather material for *The Road to Wigan Pier* he was still an erratic and ambivalent minor writer, struggling to make a living.

So what happened? Jaulmes, whose experience includes going down a coalmine in Ukraine, follows him to find out. In Wigan, he admires the men with shaven heads and 'spectacular tattoos' he sees, and the women with rings and diamantés in their ears and noses. They remind him of the ancient Picts in Roman times, in nice contrast to the penguins he had been watching in the south. Be that as it may, did Orwell have a Road to Damascus experience there? Whether the answer lies in his strong reaction to the hardships he saw and suffered among the miners or in his sudden complete loss of patience with his publisher Victor Gollancz and with conventional socialism, he was a much more fiery writer by the end of it.

On finishing *The Road to Wigan Pier*, his first hard-hitting book with a big print-run, he seized the opportunity to fight fascism. It could be argued that historical events did as much to radicalise Orwell as the inner progression of his ideas. If the Depression drove him deeper, the Spanish civil war completed the process by driving him perhaps as deep as a man can go.

In Spain, in quick succession, there was the experience of pure revolutionary spirit, that of being shot and almost killed for a good cause and that of being on the run as a demonised traitor. 'Though he has never lived in a totalitarian dictatorship,' Jaulmes writes, 'he suddenly understands its fundamental mechanisms and the essential part played in them by lies.' Orwell wrote to his friend, Cyril Connolly, on his return from Spain: 'I have seen wonderful things,' and indeed they shape the rest of his working life. Even his interlude in Morocco writing *Coming Up for Air*, which Jaulmes does not waste time looking at, can be seen as a further step, at least insofar as it shows how inadequate his old novel-writing routines were to freight what he now knew. Then came World War II. What can a benign incurable extremist do if he is too ill to fight, too lucid to enter politics and yet still alarmingly sane? For each person the answer has to be different, but for Orwell it was to support the war effort as best he could as a propagandist, then to write a fable and then, using his remaining strength to rub it in as hard as he possibly could, write a dystopian epic.

A fugitive from his own success with *Animal Farm*, which he tries to brush off as 'a bit of luck', Orwell retreats to a remote island to write his testament, and the man from the *Figaro* follows him there too. 'It is hard to find a more difficult place to get to in the British islands,' he notes, giving some details and travelogue on how he did it. His expedition coincides with an Orwell Society visit to Barnhill. He observes the members in their picturesque hiking gear, peering reverently at the haunts of 'their hero'. They are doing exactly the same as him, in fact, though he has been a lot more thorough about it than most of us.

So do we now know how Orwell got so much so right and why is he still so readable? Not really, but the steps along the way have come more sharply into focus. Jaulmes gives the last word to Quentin Kopp, the son of Orwell's commander in Spain, who says (back-translated from the French): 'He was open to the facts, and had no hesitation in changing his mind, which is quite unusual nowadays. So he wrote what he saw rather than what his various ideological positions called for.' It rings true, but so does almost the opposite: he was at his most powerful when he was writing most urgently to convince.

It is perhaps these paradoxes that still make Orwell's work compelling and *Sur les Traces de George Orwell* brings them out well. We can end with another one it examines: 'Orwellian' has become as familiar and meaningful a word as 'Machiavellian' and 'Kafkaesque', but what does it mean? Well, it means crushing tyranny when referring to a political situation and rigorous honesty when referring to a writing style. But that makes it a kind of doublespeak word, meaning *both* 'ungood' *and* good. Are the *Orwelliens* this book mentions, a group which exists in France, on the right side or the wrong one? To answer I would need to go back and check carefully, but unfortunately there is no index.

Desmond Avery,
Freelance writer

Barnill: A Novel
Norman Bissell
Luarth Press, Edinburgh, 2019 pp 255
ISBN: 978 1 -912147 87 8 (hbk)

The Orwellian *oeuvre* is forever expanding. Only recently, David Dwan offered his scintillating, philosophical reflections on Orwell's political ideas, D. J. Taylor and Dorian Lynskey have had fascinating 'biographies' of *Nineteen Eighty-Four* published to coincide with the novel's 70th anniversary. Now, Norman Bissell contributes an affectionate portrait of Orwell, the man, writer, lover, recluse and affectionate father in *Barnhill: A Novel*.

As Bissell acknowledges in his fascinating Afterword 'Writing *Barnhill*' (pp 245-251), the Australian author, Dennis Glover, had a similar idea – publishing a novel about Orwell's final years, *The Last Man in Europe*, in 2017. But Bissell is very different, adopting an original and engaging approach by imaging the inner-most thoughts of both Orwell (no simple task since he was a man full of contradictions) and his second wife, Sonia Brownell. These musings appear alongside a more conventional narrative that, in general, follows the historical record closely.

Bissell has clearly done his homework and read widely. His bibliography at the end (p. 255), for instance, includes the major biographies – by Crick, D. J. Taylor, Bowker and Colls – the slim portrait of Sonia by her friend Hilary Spurling; memoirs by T. R. Fyvel and George Woodcock; memories of the man collected by Stephen Wadhams, Audrey Coppard and Bernard Crick; studies of the writings by W. J. West and, of course, Orwell's own writings. And there is a useful timeline (pp 241-244) from November 1943 when Orwell resigns his post at the BBC and becomes literary editor at the leftist journal, *Tribune*, until his death at University College Hospital, London, on 21 January 1950, aged just 46.

The novel begins in May 1944 with Orwell lying awake in his flat on Mortimer Crescent, London alongside Eileen O'Shaughnessy, whom he had married in 1936. He muses: 'It must be about three o'clock. In the morning. I can't sleep for all these thoughts of my Hebridean island. And Eileen's snoring. ... We're winning the war now and all the little fascists will crawl back into their holes when we do. Until next time. But we've adopted some of their methods so we can win it. Like tapping phones and letter opening and lying on the radio' (p. 11).

The narrative then shifts to an argument between Orwell and Eileen over his continuing affair with his *Tribune* secretary, Sally McEwan. Eileen is deeply distressed. 'She grabbed the dinner plate and threw

REVIEW

it at him' (p. 14). This explosion serves to jolt Orwell's conscience – and he decides to stop the affair and concentrate on Eileen and their plans to adopt a baby son. After their Mortimer Crescent flat is destroyed by a Nazi bomb, the scene shifts to the Orwell's new apartment in Canonbury Square where a party of friends is celebrating both the arrival of the adopted son Richard and the publication of *Animal Farm*.

And so the narrative moves on: through an imagined fishing expedition with his eccentric friend Paul Potts; Orwell's departure for the continent to cover the final months of the Second World War for the *Observer*, his meeting at Hotel Scribe (or was it the Ritz?), in Paris, with Ernest Hemingway who lends him a gun. In Cologne, he is admitted to hospital but soon afterwards the terrible news comes by telegram: his wife has died in an operating theatre in Newcastle. So begins Orwell's search for a woman to help look after Richard.

Once settled in the remote house, Barnhill, on the Scottish island of Jura, Bissell carefully follows the record – showing Orwell juggling domestic hassles with his attempts to launch into what was to be his last novel, *Nineteen Eighty-Four* (originally titled *The Last Man in Europe*). So the incident in which Paul Potts storms off after Orwell's sister Avril burns his manuscript in the fire is recalled; so too his suspicions that David Holbrook, the friend of child-minder Susan Watson, is a communist spying on him.

The dialogue can at times sound somewhat unconvincing and over-contrived – as can, indeed, be Sonia's interior monologue. For instance, Chapter 6 begins with her pondering Orwell's invitation: 'He gave me detailed instructions of how to get to Barnhill, but I had other plans. You see, that was a very special summer for me. I'd met Maurice Merleau-Ponty in Nice in May and we seemed to get on like a proverbial house on fire. Of course, he had a wife and a young daughter, but that's never stopped a Frenchman' (p. 125).

Some of the most enjoyable scenes are when Bissell lets his imagination run completely free: as for instance, when George misses his train connection in Glasgow and spends the evening in the city. In Montrose Street, he passes a large group of women. He asks them about their work and their foreman, Robert, what it was like in the city during the war. Everyone is surprisingly friendly towards him. Later that evening he buys black pudding from a fish and chip shop: 'It was certainly different from anything else he'd ever tasted, but he reckoned he could grow to like this Glasgow Italian speciality' (p. 142). He sees children playing amongst the filth in the Gorbals. On Stockwell Street, the sound of a fiddle and accordion at the Scotia Bar tempts him inside. Here he meets Robert and Johnny, who has actually heard of *Animal Farm* and read his 'As I Please' columns in *Tribune*. Bissell, enjoying a Creative Scotland grant to help research the novel, revels in capturing the city's patter:

> 'Look, let me get ye a dram tae go wi yer pint,' Johnny said. George tried to say no, but Johnny wasn't having it. 'Jist you move up wan so ye can talk tae yer freen' (p.147).

And he follows up with this wonderful celebration of Glasgow as Orwell ponders: 'Still, it was a truly proletarian city. If there was one place where the revolution would break out, it would be Glasgow. It nearly had after the First World War when Lloyd George's government sent tanks into the city after police scattered the huge crowd of men with their red flags who were demanding a forty-hour week to create jobs for returning soldiers' (p. 151).

The drama of the near-death experience in the Corryvreckan whirlpool for Orwell, Richard and cousins Henry and Lucy is captured effectively. Amidst it all, Orwell is shown remaining stubbornly cool and nonchalant:

REVIEW

> 'Well, we must find something to eat. I'll see if I can find any birds' eggs and wood for a fire. I won't be long,' George announced as he trooped off (p. 175).

As Orwell continues bashing out his novel his health deteriorates: first he's admitted to Hairmyres Hospital near Glasgow – then to Cranham Sanatorium in the Cotswolds. With his novel delivered to the publishers, Orwell spends all his time reading:

> … everything from D. H. Lawrence to Edgar Allan Poe, *Jude the Obscure* to *New Grub Street*. He got through about three books a week since he was allowed to do little else. As time passed he read more and more of Joseph Conrad and Evelyn Waugh's work and decided to make notes on them in his notebook with the intention of writing extended essays about them. As his mood became blacker he even began reading Dante's *Divine Comedy*. He wanted to see what might lie in store for him, whether it be Heaven or Hell – or somewhere in-between (p. 204).

Finally admitted to University College Hospital, London, and just before his death, Orwell is visited by his old Etonian classics teacher Andrew Gow. This ties into a theme Bissell has developed through the novel highlighting the (usually marginalised) role of spooks in Orwell's life. At the end of the novel, Sonia ponders (perhaps improbably) the possible links between Gow and the Cambridge Soviet Spy Ring of Burgess, Maclean, Philby and Blunt (p. 234).

The close ties with intelligence of Orwell's friends David Astor, the *Observer* editor, and 'Freddie' Ayer, the celebrated philosopher, are highlighted in the novel. But Orwell's own probable involvement with intelligence is never really exploited. Thus Orwell's trip to the Continent in 1945 to report the final days of the Second World War for the *Observer* is covered, but the fact that all the men he met in Paris – Ayer, Muggeridge, Hemingway and Harold Acton – were, in some way, connected with the security services is ignored. In 1944, Astor was transferred to a unit liaising between the Special Operations Executive and the Resistance in France, helping the French underground in London spread the word to groups throughout Europe. And Orwell, perhaps inspired by Astor, actually attended in Paris the first conference of the Committee for European Federation, bringing together Resistance groups from around Europe. The celebrated French novelist and editor of *Combat*, Albert Camus, was present but fell ill just before he was due to meet Orwell. If only Bissell had imagined that meeting actually going ahead – what fun he could have had!

**Richard Lance Keeble,
University of Lincoln and Liverpool Hope University**

George Orwell Studies

Subscription information

Each volume contains two issues, published half-yearly.

Annual Subscription (including postage)

Personal Subscription

UK	£30
Europe	£33
RoW	£35

Institutional Subscription

UK	£100
Europe	£115
RoW	£120

Single Issue copies (subject to availability)

UK	£15
Europe	£17
RoW	£20

Enquiries regarding subscriptions and orders should be sent to:

    Journals Fulfilment Department
    Abramis Academic
    ASK House
    Northgate Avenue
    Bury St Edmunds
    Suffolk, IP32 6BB
    UK

Tel: +44(0)1284 700321
Email: info@abramis.co.uk

www.ingramcontent.com/pod-product-compliance
Lightning Source LLC
Chambersburg PA
CBHW080405170426
43193CB00016B/2812